Brexit and Competition Law

This book provides the first comprehensive analysis of the immediate and likely longer-term consequences of Brexit for the UK's competition law regime and includes the competition and subsidy control provisions of the EU–UK Trade and Cooperation Agreement. It has been written to be of value to scholars and practitioners of competition law, whilst also providing a useful guide to readers with only limited understanding of competition rules. The book provides a detailed critical discussion of how Brexit impacts on five key aspects of competition policy in the UK: legislation, institutions and cooperation; antitrust rules that prohibit anti-competitive agreements and the abuse of a dominant position; private enforcement, in particular actions for damages; regulation of mergers and acquisitions; and State aid or subsidy control rules.

Barry Rodger is Professor of Law at the University of Strathclyde, UK. He is the Chair and Co-Organiser of the Competition Law Scholars' Forum and Co-Editor of the *Competition Law Review*.

Andreas Stephan is Professor of Competition Law and Head of the Law School at the University of East Anglia, UK.

Legal Perspectives on Brexit
Series Editor: Richard Lang, University of Brighton, UK
Editorial Board: David Edward CMG, QC, MA, LLB, LLD, FRSE
(University of Edinburgh, UK, *Emeritus*)
Margot Horspool (University of Surrey, UK, *Emeritus*)
Shirley McDonagh (CILEx, UK)

'Legal Perspectives on Brexit' is a peer-reviewed series of short-form books which goes beyond responding to public curiosity aroused by the triggering of Article 50 to recognize the ongoing legal and political disputes Brexit has prompted. Aimed at academics and professionals it provides expert commentary on and predictions about the possible legislative and judicial implications of Brexit for each of the different sectors of regulation which have for so long been dominated by EU Law, creating a valuable one stop resource which exposes, explores and perhaps even resolves legal problems stemming from the separation of UK and EU legal systems.

Brexit and Aviation Law
Jan Walulik

Brexit and Procurement Law
Catherine Maddox

Brexit and the Car Industry
Matthew Humphreys and Doug Munro

Brexit and Competition Law
Barry Rodger and Andreas Stephan

Forthcoming

Brexit and Intellectual Property Law
Janice Denoncourt

Brexit and Energy Law
Raphael Heffron

https://www.routledge.com/law/series/BREXIT

Brexit and Competition Law

Barry Rodger and Andreas Stephan

LONDON AND NEW YORK

First published 2022
by Routledge
2 Park Square, Milton Park, Abingdon, Oxon OX14 4RN

and by Routledge
605 Third Avenue, New York, NY 10158

Routledge is an imprint of the Taylor & Francis Group, an informa business

© 2022 Andreas Stephan and Barry Rodger

British Library Cataloguing-in-Publication Data
A catalogue record for this book is available from the British Library

Library of Congress Cataloging-in-Publication Data
A catalog record has been requested for this book

ISBN: 978-1-138-47707-0 (hbk)
ISBN: 978-1-032-06748-3 (pbk)
ISBN: 978-1-351-10544-6 (ebk)

DOI: 10.4324/9781351105446

Typeset in Times New Roman
by Deanta Global Publishing Services, Chennai, India

Contents

Introduction

In the last 40 years, competition law has grown from a relatively obscure and underdeveloped legal discipline, to one of the most recognisable and significant areas of business regulation and enforcement. The UK's relationship with the European Union (EU) has been symbiotic in this journey. The competition rules of the EU, and the European Economic Community (EEC) before it, developed primarily through decades of case law, and by the 1990s they were being emulated in the domestic laws of Member States and in scores of non-EU jurisdictions which were adopting competition law for the first time.[1] This EU approach has shaped the development of competition law and policy in the UK since the late 1990s, with the passing of the Competition Act 1998, which brought domestic antitrust rules in line with those of the EU.[2] Subsequent to this, the UK played a central role in the modernisation of EU competition law, notably by championing the move towards a more economics- and effects-based approach[3] to the application of main EU competition rules and Merger Regulation controls, and in the broad convergence of competition rules internationally through its role in organisations like the International Competition Network.[4]

As a Member State, the application and enforcement of the two sets of parallel EU and UK competition rules were inextricably linked and over the

---

1 A Bradford et al., 'The Global Dominance of European Competition Law Over American Antitrust Law' (2019) 16(4) Journal of Empirical Legal Studies 731–766; MRA Palim, 'The Worldwide Growth of Competition Law: An Empirical Analysis' (1998) [Spring] Antitrust Bulletin 105.

2 B Rodger and A MacCulloch, *The UK Competition Act: A New Era for UK Competition Law* (Hart Publishing 2000); M Coleman and M Grenfell, *The Competition Act 1998: Law and Practice* (Oxford University Press 2001).

3 AC Witt, *The More Economic Approach to EU Antitrust Law* (Hart Publishing 2019).

4 www.internationalcompetitionnetwork.org (accessed 21 January 2021); P Lugard (ed), *The International Competition Network at Ten* (Intersentia 2011).

last twenty years also largely in substantive alignment. Competition law in the EU operates on a 'one-stop-shop' principle, meaning that competition cases are considered by the European Commission (as the authority for the whole of the EU) or by national competition authorities, but never both. Consequently, the Commission deals with anti-competitive conduct and mergers that are international in nature and affect more than one Member State. It leaves national competition authorities to deal with predominantly domestic cases, but also with the power to apply EU and national competition rules alongside each other. The Commission is also primarily responsible for the enforcement of State aid rules, which regulate situations where a public authority confers any advantage to businesses (usually a subsidy, tax break or loan) on a selective basis that is not on commercial terms and which may distort competition. The rules on State aid prevent subsidies that attract international investment that would otherwise have gone elsewhere in the EU, or that allow the recipient to invest more, or remain in business where they would otherwise have closed down. Subsidies are generally permitted where they pursue a specific policy objective (market failure or economic equity), but must be proportionate and the benefits must outweigh any negative effects on businesses in other Member States.

A final key characteristic of the EU regime is that the national competition authorities, tribunals and courts in applying EU competition law in their decisional practice, are generally bound and guided by the case law of the Court of Justice of the European Union (CJEU).[5] The private enforcement of competition rules is governed by the set of domestic private law rules in each Member State, and it is notable that London had become a forum of choice for European claimants (predominantly other businesses) bringing damages actions related to infringement decisions of the European Commission.[6] The act of leaving the EU has resulted in the UK becoming a third country from an EU perspective and in the Competition and Markets Authority (CMA) being transformed from an EU national competition authority, subsidiary in status to the European Commission, to potentially one of the most significant enforcers of competition law internationally.

This book provides the first comprehensive analysis of the immediate and likely longer-term consequences of Brexit for the UK's competition law regime. It has been written to be of value to researchers and practitioners of competition law by significantly furthering our knowledge in this

5 See K Cseres, 'Comparing Laws in the Enforcement of EU and National Competition Laws' (2010) 3(7) European Journal of Legal Studies 7–44.
6 M Kuijpers et al., 'Actions for Damages in the Netherlands, the United Kingdom and Germany' (2015) 6(2) Journal of Competition Law & Practice 129–142.

area, whilst also providing a useful guide to readers with only limited understanding of competition rules. The book provides a detailed critical discussion of how Brexit impacts on five key aspects of competition policy in the UK. These are (i) legislation, institutions and cooperation; (ii) antitrust rules that prohibit anti-competitive agreements and the abuse of a dominant position; (iii) private enforcement or actions for damages; (iv) regulation of mergers and acquisitions; and (v) State aid (or subsidy control) rules that regulate any advantage granted by a public authority through state resources on a selective basis (principally subsidies and tax concessions). It is this last pillar of competition policy that proved particularly contentious in the negotiations between the UK and the EU to agree on a future trading arrangement.

The remainder of this introductory chapter provides an overview of the design and purpose of competition rules, followed by an outline of the development of EU and UK competition laws respectively. There is then a chapter for each of the five aspects identified above, ending with a concluding chapter that reflects on key themes, future directions and research.

An overview of competition law

The primary purpose of competition law is to promote competition among those engaged in an economic activity (typically businesses) for the benefit of consumers. The rivalry that competition instils between businesses is generally thought to result in the best market outcomes for consumers and the economy as a whole.[7] This is because it tends to result in more outputs being produced for a lower price, while incentivising innovation and leading improved quality and choice.[8] The focus on consumers is important because they tend to be comparatively weak when dealing with sellers (which is why they also require protection from consumer law) and because the cost of anti-competitive behaviour tends to be passed down and borne by final consumers.[9] This is not to suggest that competition *always* provides the best outcome, or that government intervention in the form of market controls or nationalisation is not sometimes desirable.[10] Indeed, competition

---

7 See generally R Schmalensee and R Willig (eds) *Handbook of Industrial Organization*, Volume 1 (North-Holland 1989) and subsequent volumes.
8 M Motta, *Competition Policy: Theory and Practice* (Cambridge University Press 2004) Chapter 2.
9 ibid.
10 See discussion in A Devlin, 'Antitrust in an Era of Market Failure' (2010) 33(2) Harvard Journal of Law 557–606.

law has historically struggled to fully encapsulate values other than market efficiency and consumer welfare. With the exception of State aid rules, objectives such as environmental protection may be better realised through other tools, such as taxation, although competition law enforcement may allow for some otherwise unacceptable forms of cooperation between competitors where the end result is beneficial for society, such as enhanced sustainability.

The role of competition law is threefold. The first is to use regulation and enforcement to prevent or limit the scope for monopoly outcomes. Left to their own devices, competing firms will quickly formulate strategies for increasing their individual and/or collective profit. Their ability to do this will vary depending on the characteristics of the market. Two key elements needed for anti-competitive outcomes are high barriers to entry (it being very difficult or costly for new competitors to enter the market) and low substitutability (the product being produced and sold has few substitutes and so consumers cannot react to price increases by simply buying something else). Where these two conditions hold, major market players can exploit or leverage their market power (known as 'abuse' of dominance or monopolisation) to prevent competition, competitors can stifle competition by acting as a cartel to artificially increase prices, or competitors can merge to form larger companies that have greater control over the market. These constitute the three main areas of competition law: (i) the prohibition of abuse of a dominant position by firms with very significant market power; (ii) the prohibition of anti-competitive agreements; and (iii) the regulation of mergers and acquisitions to either prevent anti-competitive mergers or agree to countervailing remedies that protect competition.

The second role of competition law is to constrain the behaviour of government, whilst allowing interventions to deal with genuine market failure. The aforementioned competition rules generally apply to all public bodies and state-owned companies engaged in an economic activity. In relation to private businesses, governments typically face lobbying from those who want to shape regulation to suit their strategic objectives or who are seeking financial assistance in the form of subsidies or tax concessions. Where such measures are offered to everyone, they do not generally have a distortive effect. However, government assistance that is granted on a selective basis (e.g. to one company or one geographical region) can distort competition by undermining the benefits of rivalry, for example where that assistance helps a failing and inefficient firm, or diverts investment away from more efficient and beneficial use elsewhere. It also risks triggering a costly subsidy war between governments keen to support their own 'national champions'. EU State aid rules and World Trade Organization (WTO) rules on subsidy control aim to constrain these wasteful uses of public money, whilst allowing governments to deal with genuine market failure.[11] This is where competition has failed to provide the supply, quality or affordability that is needed to fulfil an important set of needs for society. It is here that government controls, sector-specific regulation, or nationalisation may be desirable.

The third role of competition law is to facilitate compensation for those harmed by anti-competitive behaviour. This may be driven predominantly by restorative justice and the need to compensate consumers (who are often other businesses). The purpose is to return those parties who have suffered harm or loss as a result of anti-competitive behaviour to a situation equivalent to if they had not suffered the harm.[12] The compensation-based approach has underscored a range of legal initiatives to facilitate private enforcement in the EU.[13] Private enforcement of competition law can also be driven predominantly by deterrence, by allowing parties to recover over and beyond the actual harm they suffered (i.e. punitive damages). A deterrence-based approach is at the core of the rules facilitating antitrust litigation in the United States, exemplified by the rule allowing antitrust claimants to pursue three times the harm suffered (so-called 'treble damages' actions). Actions for damages also play a role in the context of State aid, where companies can bring an action against the government of an EU Member State for compensation in connection with unlawful and distortive aid granted to a competitor.

The development of EU competition law

Competition law of the EU has its origins in the European Coal and Steel Community established in 1951. This set up a centralised authority for the regulation of industrial production in Belgium, France, Italy, Luxembourg, the Netherlands and West Germany in order to avoid future conflict in Europe. It included competition provisions relating to agreements, dominance and merger control (Articles 60 and 65–66). For reasons that are not entirely certain, only the first two of these found expression in the Treaty of Rome (1958–1999), which established the EEC and aimed to transform the conditions of trade and production between its six members.

---

11 On EU State aid, see E Stuart, *Sixty Years of EU State aid Law and Policy* (Kluwer 2018). On WTO, see BM Hoekman and PC Mavroidis, *The World Trade Organization: Law, Economics and Politics*, 2nd ed (Routledge 2015) Chapter 3.

12 C Argenton, D Geradin and A Stephan, *EU Cartel Law and Economics* (Oxford University Press 2021) Chapter 6.

13 B Rodger (ed), *Competition Law Comparative Private Enforcement and Collective Redress across the EU* (Kluwer 2014).

This included eliminating trade barriers and ensuing fair competition. The provisions were carried over into the European Communities Treaty (1999–2009) and are now found in the Treaty on the Functioning of the European Union (TFEU). These articles are:

- *Article 101 TFEU* – the prohibition of anti-competitive agreements between undertakings, decisions by associations of undertakings and concerted practices which may affect trade between Member States and which have as their object or effect the prevention, restriction or distortion of competition.
- *Article 102 TFEU* – the prohibition of an abuse of a dominant position within the internal market or in a substantial part of it, in so far as it may affect trade between Member States.

In addition to these, Articles 107–8 TFEU carried over rules on control of State aid, which give the European Commission the power to review, abolish or alter aid that is incompatible with the internal market. Rules to control mergers and acquisitions (known as 'concentrations' in EU law) on competition grounds did not come about until Council Regulation (EEC) No 4064/89 of 21 December 1989 and are now set out in Council Regulation (EC) No 139/2004 of 20 January 2004.

The original purpose of these rules (along with the many other objectives set out in the treaties) was to promote the creation of a common market by constraining behaviour that might fragment trade between Member States. Indeed, market integration has occasionally shaped competition law in ways that trump the competitive dynamic or notions of efficiency in economics. An example of this is the prohibition of export bans in the context of Article 101, as it applies to agreements between manufacturers and distributors in different Member States. Agreeing that those distributors cannot sell to consumers in other Member States can provide a very strong incentive for those firms to promote the manufacturer's products and successfully launch them to market. Yet it is prohibited (at least in its strictest form), because it also has the effect of fragmenting or 'compartmentalising' the common market along national lines.

In the early days of European competition law enforcement, following the introduction of Regulation 17/62, which provided the core roles for enforcing the treaty rules on competition, there was a lot of uncertainty as to how those rules applied or would be enforced. The boundaries of EU competition law and its practical application have developed primarily through the decisional practice of the European Commission and the case law ('jurisprudence') of the European courts, notably the CJEU. The General Court hears appeals from businesses subject to the enforcement decisions of the European Commission and from Member States who wish to challenge Commission decisions relating to State aid. The General Court's decisions can be appealed to the CJEU for final review. Moreover, the CJEU has developed key competition law principles using its interpretative function in delivering preliminary rulings on requests from the national courts.[14] Many aspects of EU competition law are very much continuing to evolve and grow, which is why the fact that the EU and UK rules were consistent with each other at the point of Brexit does not necessarily mean they will remain so over time.

The boundaries of Article 101 and 102 continue to develop and it is notable that the first Article 102 abuse of dominance case was not until the 1970s. There is a vast range of commercial arrangements which may potentially be caught by these EU competition law rules, and their scope is deliberately wide so as to prevent firms from easily circumventing them. Greater legal certainty has been provided by the introduction of block exemption regulations, which provide safe harbours from liability where certain criteria have been met. Among the most important block exemptions in this respect are those relating to horizontal cooperation agreements such as for research and development, vertical agreements dealing with exclusive dealing and distribution, and the block exemption relating to certain forms of State aid. The CJEU and the Commission have also sought to empower private individuals and businesses with the ability to enforce competition law and seek remedies including injunctive relief and damages, notably through Directive 2014/104/EU, which seeks to remove barriers to bringing actions for damages under national law within EU Member States. Finally, the Commission has sought to shift EU competition law to a more economics-based enforcement approach, in relation to vertical agreements, abuse of dominance and merger control. State aid too has undergone its own process of modernisation.

The development of UK competition law

The development of UK competition law has been very different. Following the Second World War and even after it became a member of the EEC, the UK did not seek to promote competition through rules of prohibition. For decades, anti-competitive agreements and mergers rarely received more than a regulatory slap on the wrist. For example, cartel agreements within the UK were long subject to mandatory public registration and would only

---

14 See for example B Rodger, *Article 234 and Competition Law: A Comparative Analysis* (Kluwer Law International 2008).

be prohibited if found to be against public interest.[15] When the UK joined the EEC in 1973 it became subject to EU rules on agreements, abuse of dominance and State aid, where they had an effect on trade between Member States. Yet its domestic enforcement regime retained the registration system for anti-competitive agreements and an equally weak regime against exploitative and exclusionary behaviour.[16] There was no prohibition of abusive conduct, but simply a monopoly investigations system based on public interest and allowing for prospective remedies but no sanctions. Public interest was also central to merger control, leading to some periods of unpredictable and inconsistent decision-making.[17] This period was also marked by very significant political involvement in competition law, which very much took a back seat to the interventionist industrial policies of the 1960s and 1970s. It was during the 1980s that the weaknesses in this approach began to be recognised, as did the need to develop a competition law enforcement regime more in line with that of the EEC and the United States.

This shift in approach came about with the Competition Act 1998 and Enterprise Act 2002. These important pieces of legislation aligned UK competition law to EU law by creating domestic equivalents to Article 101 and 102 and adopting an economics-based system of merger control similar to that being developed by the EU at the time. These two Acts resulted in very significant institutional changes, in particular the creation of a competition authority independent of direct government control (the Office of Fair Trading, now merged with the Competition Commission as the Competition and Markets Authority following the Enterprise and Regulatory Reform Act 2013), by giving competition powers to sector-specific regulators and by creating the Competition Appeals Tribunal – a specialist body to hear appeals in competition cases.[18] The involvement of government in merger

---

15 Restrictive Trade Practices Acts of 1956 and 1968. Referrals were made by the Registrar and later the Office of Fair Trading. See B Lyons, D Reader and A Stephan, 'UK Competition Policy Post-Brexit: Taking Back Control While Resisting the Siren Calls' (2017) 5(3) Journal of Antitrust Enforcement 347–374.

16 Restrictive Trade Practices Act 1976. See R Clarke, S Davies and N Driffield, *Monopoly Policy in the UK: Assessing the Evidence* (Edward Elgar 1998) p. 16.

17 See generally SRM Wilks, *In the Public Interest: Competition Policy and the Monopolies and Mergers Commission* (Manchester University Press 1999).

18 See B Rodger and A MacCulloch, *The UK Competition Act: A New Era for UK Competition Law* (Hart Publishing 2000); and N Dunne, 'Concurrency' in A MacCulloch, B Rodger and P Whelan (eds), *The UK Competition Regime: A Twenty-Year Retrospective* (Oxford University Press 2021). Concurrent competition law powers are also held by the following sector-specific regulators, who hold them 'concurrently' with the CMA: Civil Aviation Authority (CAA), Financial Conduct Authority (FCA), Gas and Electricity Markets Authority (Ofgem), Northern Ireland Authority for Utility Regulation (NIAUR), Office of

regulation was restricted to a limited set of interventions on public interest grounds, such as national security. The Competition Act also introduced new investigative powers and penalties that brought the UK into line with the antitrust laws of the EU and many other jurisdictions, and allowed for infringement decisions under either the Act or under EU law (whether delivered by the Commission or the CMA) to be used in support of follow-on actions and damages claims.[19] Indeed, the UK went further than simply emulating the EU system, as the Enterprise Act 2002 also created the power to break up firms when market investigations find competition is not working properly. That Act also criminalised the involvement of individuals in the most serious forms of cartel conduct and amended the Directors Disqualification Act 1986 to enable the CMA to seek disqualification orders (a civil penalty) against directors of companies that have been found to have infringed competition law.[20]

Accordingly, the following sets of competition law rules were potentially applicable in the UK before Brexit:

At the EU level

- Articles 101 and 102, potentially enforced by either the Commission or by National Competition Authorities (including the CMA) where their conduct had an effect on inter-state trade.
- The EU Merger Regulation 139/2004 when involved in a Community dimension merger.
- The EU State aid rules, principally enforced by the Commission.

At the UK level

- The Competition Act 1998 Chapter I and II prohibitions. These were modelled on Articles 101 and 102 and with a requirement under s.60 of the Competition Act to interpret them consistently with their EU law equivalents, as interpreted by the CJEU in particular.
- The merger control rules under the Enterprise Act, where applicable, and only (with limited exceptions) where the merger was not of

---

Communications (Ofcom), Office of Rail and Road (ORR), Payment Systems Regulator (PSR), and the Water Services Regulation Authority (Ofwat).

19 The ability to bring actions for damages was enhanced by the Consumer Rights Act 2015, which includes the ability to bring opt-out collective actions.

20 Enterprise Act 2002, Part 4 (Market Investigations), s.188 (Cartel Offence), and s.204 (Directors Disqualification).

a Community dimension and therefore did not fall within Regulation 139/2004.

• The market investigations provisions of the Enterprise Act 2002. The application of these rules, formerly monopoly investigations under the old traditional Fair Trading Act 1973 regime, have been left unscathed by withdrawal from the EU and will not be discussed further in this book.

It is worth noting that s.60 of the Competition Act 1998 was not mandated by EU law. The UK legislator voluntarily took this approach on the basis that the EU rules would enhance deterrence. Ironically, it also felt that harmonised rules would be beneficial to avoid double regulatory burdens on businesses having to comply with two sets of different competition rules.[21]

This book will chart how these existing sets of competition rules and their enforcement have changed and are likely to develop as a result of UK withdrawal from the European Union.

There has been no suggestion that either jurisdiction will seek to move backwards in terms of policy. Indeed, the harmonising of EU and UK competition law coincided with a trend across all EU Member States and much of the world, in terms of converging institutional and substantive rules. Yet this brief history is important in demonstrating how rapidly EU and UK competition law has evolved and continues to evolve. It is not a legal discipline that stands still for very long and that context is important for much of the discussion in this book.

---

21 See R Whish, 'The Competition Act 1998 and the Prior Debate on Reform' in B Rodger and A MacCulloch (eds), *The Competition Act 1998: A New Era for UK Competition Law* (Hart Publishing, 2000) Chapter 1.

1 Legislation, institutions and cooperation

To understand the full consequences of Brexit for the UK's competition law regime, it is necessary to consider the impact on the law itself, on the institutions responsible for enforcing it and on cooperation with competition authorities in the EU and beyond. This chapter first identifies some of the immediate consequences for each of the five substantive areas of competition enforcement: anti-competitive agreements, abuse of dominance, private enforcement, merger control and State aid. It will be shown that – with the exception of State aid – the UK regime was reasonably well placed to transition to a post-Brexit world with minimal disruption to businesses or markets. However, Brexit does create some practical challenges and uncertainties for businesses that operate in both the UK and the EU, and there is significant scope for divergence of rules in the longer term. These issues and others will be expanded on in Chapters 2–5, where we discuss each area of enforcement in far greater detail. State aid proved to be particularly contentious because, unlike the other four areas, there was no UK State aid regime in place by the end of the transitionary period.

The chapter then focuses on the institutions responsible for enforcing competition law and in particular on the Competition and Markets Authority (CMA). Brexit creates particular institutional challenges for the CMA, as it is elevated from the national competition authority of an EU Member State focused on domestic cases to an authority responsible for protecting UK markets from all anti-competitive conduct, whether domestic or international. As we shall see, this creates immediate challenges relating to capacity, resourcing and cooperation. The transition to its new status as a non-EU, third-country regulator means the CMA faces both a significantly increased workload and the loss of important information-sharing that exists between the national authorities of EU Member States. Yet it also means the UK has greater freedom to design and enforce competition law in the interests of

DOI: 10.4324/9781351105446-1

UK markets and consumers, where such divergence would not have been feasible or permitted as an EU Member State.[1]

1.1 Substantive rules

As was explained in the Introduction, the Competition Act 1998 essentially incorporated Articles 101 and 102 of the Treaty on the Functioning of the European Union (TFEU) into domestic law, and there was no practical distinction between the two sets of provisions, beyond jurisdiction.[2] Indeed consistency between them was ensured by the Competition Act 1998, s.60, which required that

> so far as is possible [...], questions arising [in relation to the investigation and enforcement of UK competition law] are dealt with in a manner which is consistent with the treatment of corresponding questions arising in Community Law.

Consistency between European Union (EU) and national competition law is also governed by Regulation 1/2003, which creates certain obligations designed to ensure Articles 101 and 102 are 'applied effectively and uniformly in the Community'.[3] Regulation 1 was part of a drive to modernise EU competition law by allowing national authorities and courts to apply the two EU law treaty provisions in full for the first time,[4] although generally pan-European anti-competitive behaviour would fall under the exclusive competence of the European Commission on behalf of all Member States.[5] However, where the Competition and Markets Authority (CMA) (in a similar way as other Member States' national competition authorities) initiated proceedings in an enforcement case that was not investigated by

---

1 In February 2021 an independent review of the UK's competition regime was published, but this did not recommend any significant departure from the UK's current approach. See: Power To The People: Stronger Consumer Choice and Competition So Markets Work for People, Not the Other Way Around – An Independent Report Presented to Her Majesty's Government by John Penrose MP (February 2021).

2 Ben Rayment, 'The Consistency Principle: Section 60 of the Competition Act 1998' in B Rodger (ed), *Ten Years of UK Competition Law Reform* (Edinburgh University Press 2010) Chapter 4.

3 Council Regulation (EC) 1/2003 of 16 December 2002 on the implementation of the rules on competition laid down in Articles 81 and 82 of the Treaty [2003] OJ L 1/1, recital 1.

4 The Commission previously held exclusive responsibility for the granting of exemptions under Article 101(3) through a notification system. This was replaced by a self-assessed exception regime, but there was anxiety about how 101(3) in particular would be applied at the national level. See Case C-344/98, *Masterfoods v. HB Ice Cream*, Judgement of the European Court of Justice of 14 December 2000 [2000] ECR I-11369.

5 Council Regulation (EC) 1/2003, Article 3(1).

the Commission, but which may also affect trade between Member States, it was under an obligation to apply either Article 101 or 102 TFEU, in addition to the Competition Act 1998.[6] Moreover, Chapter I of the 1998 Act could not prohibit agreements that did not amount to infringements of Article 101(1) or which fulfilled the conditions of the efficiency exception contained in Article 101(3).[7] Chapter II, on the other hand, could be stricter than Article 102. The practical consequence of Regulation 1/2003 was that UK authorities and courts were largely bound by the jurisprudence of the Court of Justice of the European Union (CJEU) and decisional practice of the Commission, so there was little substantive difference in cases whether Articles 101/102 or their UK domestic equivalents were being applied. Indeed, UK competition cases typically made reference to both, even where there was only a very limited possibility that the conduct could affect trade between Member States.

However, the relationship between EU and the UK merger enforcement regimes is different in that they are not overlapping, but where EU merger control applies it precludes the exercise of national merger control rules. Moreover, the substantive tests are different in that the European Commission may block mergers that lead to a *significant impediment to effective competition,*[8] whereas the CMA focuses on a *substantial lessening of competition.*[9] Nevertheless, the thrust of merger control at the EU and UK level is economics-based and so the theories of harm are the same (coordinated and uncoordinated effects), as is the economic analysis that is employed. This is not to suggest that outcomes will always be identical, but there is certainly a high level of convergence between the two. The private enforcement of competition law has always depended primarily on the domestic laws of each EU Member State – there is no EU set of private law rules as such. Nonetheless, Brexit does have an impact on the scope of private enforcement in the UK, as claimants will no longer be able to rely on decisions of the European Commission to establish the existence of an infringement, in relation to cases opened after 31 December 2020.[10] Finally, there was no UK domestic State aid regime that mirrored Articles 107 and 108 and, as will be discussed in Chapter 5, this proved to be particularly contentious when the UK and EU were negotiating their future trading relationship.

6 ibid, Article 11(6).
7 ibid, Article 3(2).
8 Council Regulation (EC) No 139/2004 of 20 January 2004 on the Control of Concentrations between Undertakings OJ [2004] L 024, Articles 2(2) and (3).
9 Enterprise Act 2002, Part 3, Chapter 1.
10 See generally 'Agreement on the Withdrawal of the United Kingdom of Great Britain and Northern Ireland from the European Union and the European Atomic Energy Community' OJ [2019] C 384, Chapter 2.

As a consequence of Brexit, the provisions contained in the Competition Act 1998 (anti-competitive agreements and abuse of dominance) and the Enterprise Act 2002 (mergers that lead to a substantial lessening of competition) essentially became 'scaled up' in their application to capture enforcement and regulation previously undertaken by the European Commission on the UK's behalf. While the CMA did occasionally investigate cases with an international dimension, the vast majority of anti-competitive conduct and merger situations that affected more than one Member State (including the UK) were dealt with by the European Commission on behalf of the EU as a whole. There is a mechanism under which a request can be made for a merger caught by the EU Merger Regulation (EUMR) to be considered at the Member State level (for example where its impact will be mainly felt in that Member State) and vice versa, but it is rarely used.[11]

When the UK voted to leave the European Union in June 2016, many scholars speculated that little would change in the relationship between UK and EU competition law, as described earlier. This is because it was thought the most likely outcome was for the UK to leave the EU but remain a member of the European Economic Area (EEA).[12] It was argued that membership in the EEA would allow the UK to continue benefiting from being in the single market, while also having the freedom to pursue its own policies on trade, fisheries, home affairs and agriculture. In the context of competition law, Articles 53 and 54 of the EEA Agreement directly mirror Articles 101 and 102 of the TFEU. Indeed, in its application of both antitrust and merger control, the European Commission's jurisdiction extends to the EU and the EEA, where the arrangement or merger has an EU and EEA dimension.[13] EEA Members are also subject to the same State aid rules and the de facto jurisdiction of the CJEU.[14] Accordingly, had the UK decided to remain

11 EU Merger Regulation, Article 9. A request can also be made by one of the merger parties prior to notification to the Commission under Article 4(4) and a request can also be made by the Secretary of State, where the protection of national legitimate interests may be at stake, under Article 21(4) of the EU Merger Regulation and Article 346 TFEU. On 31 December 2020 there was only one live Article 9 request from the UK that had been made on 8 October 2020: CMA, Joint Venture between Liberty Global Plc and Telefónica S.A. – Request pursuant to Article 9(2) of Council Regulation (EU) 139/2004. (2020) COMP/M9871.

12 For example A MacGregor and A Kidane, 'Post-Brexit Scenarios for UK Competition Policy and Public Enforcement: The EEA Model v Complete Independence' (2016) 22(4) International Trade Law and Regulation 81–90.

13 This means the arrangement, conduct or merger affects more than one EU or EEA member; see EEA Agreement [1994] OJ L1/1, Articles 55–57. Where cases have an EEA-only dimension, they are dealt with by the EFTA Surveillance Authority and the EFTA Court.

14 ibid, Articles 61–64. Article 61 is the equivalent of Article 107 TFEU. On the status of CJEU jurisprudence, Article 105(2) of the EEA Agreement states: 'The EEA Joint Committee shall keep under constant review the development of the case law of the Court of Justice

an EEA member, there would have been no material change to the scope and application of the respective rules in relation to agreements, abuse of dominance, merger control or State aid. It quickly became clear, however, that both the governments of Theresa May and of Boris Johnson felt such an outcome would not respect the referendum result. Ending free movement of people and ending the jurisdiction of the CJEU became particular political imperatives.[15] Remaining in the EU Customs Union was equally unacceptable politically, because it would have meant no freedom to forge trade deals and some continued obligation to follow EU rules involving oversight of the CJEU.[16]

Instead, the Withdrawal Agreement and the EU–UK Trade and Cooperation Agreement (TCA),[17] agreed only a week before the end of the transition period, meant a more decisive break with the EU, including the complete severance of UK from EU law, except as it relates to some aspects of law in Northern Ireland.[18] The TCA contains an obligation to maintain a competition law regime in relation to anti-competitive agreements, abuse of dominance and anti-competitive mergers, as well as an independent competition authority.[19] Apart from certain exceptions and caveats relating to specific industries, the agreement contains no detail on how these laws should be designed, or any minimum requirements. Nor is the relevant chapter subject to dispute settlement, which suggests there is little to prevent the two competition law regimes from diverging over time. As discussed later in this chapter and in Chapter 5, State aid (referred to as 'Subsidy Control' in the TCA) was a major sticking point in the negotiations relating to the 'level playing field', resulting in far more prescriptive provisions that are subject to dispute settlement (including retaliatory measures) and which closely mirror Article 107.[20] Nevertheless, there is nothing in the TCA that puts UK competition law (with the exception of State aid in relation to goods and the

of the European Communities and the EFTA Court. To this end, judgments of these courts shall be transmitted to the EEA Joint Committee which shall act as to preserve the homogenous interpretation of the Agreement'. In addition, Protocol 34 to the EEA Agreement allows the EFTA Court to ask the CJEU to decide on the interpretation of an EEA rule.

15 See for example Prime Minister Theresa May's 'Mansion House Speech' on the future economic partnership with the European Union (2 March 2018).

16 See for example Decision 1/95 of the EC-Turkey Association Council of 22 December 1995 on Implementing the Final Phase of the Customs Union [1996] OJ L 35/1, Article 66.

17 Trade and Cooperation Agreement Between the European Union and the European Atomic Energy Community, of the one part, and the United Kingdom of Great Britain and Northern Ireland, of the other part. OJ [2020] L 444/14, Title XI: Level Playing Field for Open and Fair Competition and Sustainable Development.

18 See HM Government Policy Paper, *The Northern Ireland Protocol* (10 December 2020).

19 TCA, Chapter 2 of Title XI.

20 TCA, Chapter 3 of Title XI.

electricity market in Northern Ireland) directly under the jurisdiction of the CJEU or which creates an obligation to continue to follow EU law.

With this overview of the two competition law regimes, their histories, the political context and the TCA, we now turn to the immediate consequences for each of the five substantive areas of competition law. For these purposes we discuss anti-competitive agreements and abuse of dominance together, as 'antitrust rules'. Each of these five sections has a corresponding chapter in this book, where we examine these issues in greater detail and also consider some of the longer-term consequences.

1.1.1 Antitrust rules (Chapter 2)

The UK's two antitrust provisions are contained in Chapters I and II of the Competition Act 1998 and these are the domestic equivalents of Articles 101 and 102 TFEU. After the Brexit transition period ended, these automatically applied to all anti-competitive agreements and abuse of dominance that 'may affect trade within the United Kingdom', regardless of whether they were domestic or international.[21] No changes were necessary to the wording of the prohibitions themselves, but a statutory instrument was needed to remove key references to EU competition law.[22] The most important of these changes was the revocation of s.60, which dispensed with the obligation for UK competition law to be consistent with the law of the EU. This was replaced by s.60A, which only requires the CMA and courts to avoid inconsistency with EU law and the decisions of the CJEU before 1 January 2021, and even then, as discussed in Chapter 2, with flexibility to depart from those principles and decisions in certain appropriate circumstances. The 1998 Act was also amended to remove the many references it contained to the EU's laws and institutions, or otherwise limiting their relevance. For example terms such as 'before exit day' have been inserted to distinguish decisions initiated before the end of the transition period. Similar changes were also made to the Enterprise Act, although references to the EU were more limited by comparison. Key EU block exemption regulations were retained and adopted into UK law, but with

---

21 Competition Act 1998, s.2 and s.18. Although some confusion may be created by the requirement that Chapter I be 'implemented in the United Kingdom'. See J Fingleton et al., 'The Implications of Brexit for UK Competition Law and Policy' (2017) 13(3) Journal of Competition Law and Economics 389–422.

22 See Statutory Instrument, Exiting the European Union: Competition, The Competition (Amendment etc.) (EU Exit) Regulations 2019.

the ability for the Secretary of State (on recommendation of the CMA) to vary or revoke these.

The design and application of the UK's antitrust rules have therefore remained essentially unchanged, but now apply to all anti-competitive behaviour that affects trade in the UK. Chapter 2 of this book will focus on the more contentious issue of the extent to which UK and EU antitrust enforcement will remain aligned in the future. The status of EU case law is of particular importance, as the combination of the Competition Act provisions being based on Articles 101 and 102, and the consistency principle set out in s.60, have meant that the UK's domestic competition case law has been heavily reliant on EU jurisprudence.[23] The CMA and the specialist Competition Appeals Tribunal (CAT) have, in interpreting and applying the domestic rules, expressly followed Commission decisions and the case law of the CJEU.[24] In developing domestic rules in the future, consequent to the new revised s.60A of the Act, there is scope for the UK courts and authorities to diverge from EU law precedent and there will be no obligation to follow any future EU case law developments that are not considered to be suitable for UK markets.

1.1.2 Private enforcement (Chapter 3)

While the UK's membership of the EU limited its ability to pursue international anti-competitive behaviour through *public* enforcement, the courts in London (the High Court and more recently the CAT) developed as the forum of choice for *private* follow-on actions for damages in EU cartel cases. This means that UK and foreign claimants were assisted by the provision under European law, allowing them to rely on a European Commission decision to establish that there was a breach of competition law. While these actions are likely to continue for some years[25] by virtue of the fact that rights derived before Brexit will continue to be recognised by UK law, uncertainty surrounds the scope for follow-on actions for competition law breaches that occurred *after* the UK broke ties with the EU.[26] Brexit has meant that s.47A

---

23 See generally B Rodger (ed), *Ten Years of UK Competition Law Reform* (Edinburgh University Press 2010); and B Rodger, P Whelan and A MacCulloch (eds), *The UK Competition Law Regime: A Twenty-Year Retrospective* (Oxford University Press 2021).

24 Whether in the CJEU's capacity as an appeal court or in giving preliminary rulings.

25 Article 86(1) of the Withdrawal Agreement states that all cases *pending* before the CJEU at the end of the transition period will fall within the CJEU's jurisdiction until they are finalised. This includes decisions on appeals.

26 See Statutory Instrument, Exiting the European Union: Competition, The Competition (Amendment etc.) (EU Exit) Regulations 2019, Part 6 at 14.

and s.58A of the 1998 Act have been amended to remove the provision that allowed follow-on actions that rely on infringement decisions by the European Commission.[27] This means that a UK claimant seeking damages for a cartel that was subject to an infringement decision by the Commission and not the CMA may need to prove substantive liability before UK courts, and this may be particularly challenging in long-standing, complex and secret cartels. However, European infringement decisions may still carry some weight in helping claimants establish the existence of an infringement. The problem may be alleviated by the CMA adopting parallel decisions relating to the same conduct, but this may not help claimants who did not predominantly suffer harm in the UK or cases that did not affect UK markets at all.[28] They are more likely to simply pursue their action in an EU Member State. These issues surrounding the impact on private enforcement post-Brexit shall be discussed in greater detail in Chapter 3.

1.1.3 Merger rules (Chapter 4)

As with antitrust rules, the substance of the UK's merger control regime remained unchanged as a result of Brexit. The question of whether a merger had a *community dimension* – which would, pre-Brexit, have precluded the application of the UK merger control process – simply became irrelevant, and the UK merger rules became applicable to all merger situations that met the UK's merger regulation thresholds. An obvious consequence of this is that the EU's one-stop-shop merger control by the Commission no longer applies in the UK and consequently firms operating in both jurisdictions must have any proposed merger cleared by both regulators, where previously a merger would be reviewed by either the Commission or the CMA. Chapter 4 of this book will focus on the consequences of requiring two sets of regulatory clearance for mergers, as opposed to a single approval process. For example, the relevant turnover thresholds of the UK and the EU were designed to take into account the fact the UK was a Member State. Consequently, the current threshold for a UK-qualifying merger may need to be adjusted upwards to reflect the CMA's new international workload, and the EU threshold may need to be adjusted downwards to reflect that it will no longer capture turnover in the UK. In addition, there may be a prospect of diverging merger review process outcomes, where there are different

---

27 ibid.
28 See discussion of submitted evidence in House of Lords European Union Committee, *Brexit: Competition and State Aid*, 12th Report of Session 2017–19 (2 February 2018) HL Paper 67, paras 62–70.

assessments of the potential competition effects. Divergence will be significantly more likely if either the UK or EU makes greater use of interventions on grounds such as industrial policy, environment or other wider public interest issues. Such interventions might result in a merger that raises no competition concerns being blocked. Moreover, it could result in a merger being approved despite raising serious competition concerns.[29]

1.1.4 State aid rules (Chapter 5)

In contrast to antitrust and merger control, the UK had no national State aid regime as a member of the European Union.[30] The European Commission was responsible for reviewing aid granted by a UK public authority under the EU's system of ex ante notification and clearance. It had the power to alter or prohibit UK State aid that did not benefit from the general block exemption regulation (that provides a safe harbour for types of State aid that are likely to be beneficial) and was incompatible with Article 107 TFEU.[31] Under the original Withdrawal Agreement negotiated by the government of Theresa May, the UK was under an obligation to continue being subject to State aid rules, as part of the so-called Northern Ireland backstop. This plan was scrapped by the government of Boris Johnson and these provisions were excluded from the revised agreement.[32] Nevertheless, the EU's negotiating position in March 2020 continued to be that the UK should follow EU State aid rules, while the UK preferred a reporting system based on World Trade Organization (WTO) rules on subsidies.[33] In fact, the UK's position on State aid was largely unclear for much of 2020, as a domestic regime administered by the CMA was first mooted and then kept under review pending the outcome of the trade negotiations.[34] It is unclear whether this was a negotiating tactic, but some kind of domestic subsidy control regime was widely anticipated to deal with the significant repatriation of spending

---

29 An example of this was the merger of Lloyds TSB and HBOS during the 2007 financial crisis. See A Stephan, 'Did Lloyds/HBOS Mark the Failure of an Enduring Economics-Based System of Merger Regulation?' (2011) 62(4) Northern Ireland Legal Quarterly 539–552.
30 G Peretz, 'A Star Is Torn: Brexit and State Aid' (2016) 3 European State Aid Law Quarterly 334–337.
31 Commission Regulation (EU) No 651/2014 of 17 June 2014.
32 House of Commons Briefing Paper, *The October 2019 EU-UK Withdrawal Agreement*, No CBP 8713, 17 October 2019, p. 48.
33 European Commission, *Draft Text of the Agreement on the New Partnership with the United Kingdom* (18 March 2020), UKTF (2020) 14, at Chapter 2, Section 2.
34 See 'UK Will Not Finalise State Aid Plan Until 2021' *Financial Times* (9 September 2020).

that was previously administered under the five European Structural and Investment Funds.[35]

The TCA that finally emerged constituted a significant compromise on State aid by both sides.[36] The UK is not bound by EU State aid rules and is not under the jurisdiction of the CJEU, except in relation to goods affecting trade between the EU and Northern Ireland.[37] Neither is it obliged to replicate the EU's system of ex ante notification and clearance of subsidies. Instead, it must apply a set of principles that closely mirror EU State aid rules, establish an independent authority with an 'appropriate role' and publish outline details of subsidies on an official website, alongside a justification in terms of key principles. The UK and EU can request to intervene in each other's proceedings as a third party. A Specialised Committee on the Level Playing Field is available to help resolve disputes informally. However, if either side still feels aggrieved, they may unilaterally and rapidly take remedial measures (e.g. impose tariffs) in advance of a binding arbitration tribunal process.

1.2 Institutions and cooperation

Before we delve into the issues central to each of these key areas of competition law in fuller detail, it is important to consider the implications of Brexit for institutions and cooperation. The UK's departure from the EU fundamentally changed the role of UK institutions responsible for applying competition rules and their cooperation with other jurisdictions. There are opportunities and challenges posed by the scaling up of the UK's competition law regime in becoming a fully independent competition agency at a global level. We shall also address the loss of cooperation with European partners that is a consequence of leaving the EU, and consider the potential to strengthen bilateral cooperation with agencies beyond the EU.

---

35 These are the European regional development fund, European social fund, Cohesion fund, European agricultural fund for rural development and the European maritime and fisheries fund. See K Henry and M Morris, *Regional Funding After Brexit: Opportunities for the UK's Shared Prosperity Fund* (February 2019), Institute for Public Policy Research.

36 Trade and Cooperation Agreement Between the European Union and the European Atomic Energy Community, of the one part, and the United Kingdom of Great Britain and Northern Ireland, of the other part. OJ [2020] L 444/14, Chapter 3 of Title XI: Level Playing Field For Open and Fair Competition and Sustainable Development.

37 Northern Ireland enjoys a special status in order to avoid the need for a hard border with the EU on the Island of Ireland. See Protocol on Ireland/Northern Ireland (2019), Article 10.

1.2.1 The CMA's transformed role

While the UK was a member of the EU, the CMA had the status of a national competition authority for the purposes of EU competition law.[38] Its responsibilities in relation to both UK and EU competition law included:

1. Investigating mergers which could restrict competition in the UK, but which did not meet the thresholds for the EUMR.
2. Investigating potential breaches of UK or EU prohibitions of anticompetitive agreements, abuse of dominance and of the UK criminal cartel offence.
3. Conducting market studies and investigations in UK markets where there may be competition and consumer problems (a UK-only policy tool).
4. Enforcing consumer law and considering certain regulatory references and appeals (outside the scope of this book).

The loss of EU membership will result in a significant amount of duplication of work by the European Commission and the CMA, where previously cases were dealt with by one authority but never both. This is likely to include the vast majority of potential UK competition law infringements also investigated by the European Commission, given the size of the UK economy and its overlap with EU Member States. There may also be cases that primarily affect UK markets that the European Commission will no longer prioritise, as its focus turns only to competition in the remaining 27 Member States.[39] Finally, the TCA requires the UK to implement a domestic system of subsidy control that must be overseen by an appropriate body, as discussed in Chapter 5. However, the most significant increase in terms of case work and resources will relate to merger control. Proposed mergers involving parties with considerable business interests and turnover (that meet the requisite thresholds) in the UK and across the EU will have to clear both regulatory regimes, where previously they would have been subject to a 'one stop shop' review process. The CMA estimated that its merger caseload after Brexit was likely to increase by between 60–87% based on the financial year ending 31 March 2017.[40] While the UK and EU merger

---

38 Regulation 1/2003, Article 11.
39 On priority setting in competition enforcement, see O Brook, 'Priority Setting as a Double-Edged Sword: How Modernization Strengthened the Role of Public Policy' (2020) 16(4) Journal of Competition Law & Economics 435–487.
40 Written evidence from the Competition and Markets Authority (CMP0002), reported in House of Lords European Union Committee, *Brexit: Competition and State Aid*, 12th Report of Session 2017–19 (2 February 2018) HL Paper 67, para 73.

clearance procedures will usually operate in parallel, synergies in terms of the process and the burden on businesses may be limited. This is because the UK and EU merger regimes work under different timelines and procedures (most notably there being no duty on firms to notify the CMA of a merger, as compared to the mandatory notification requirement under the EUMR).

In the context of cartel enforcement, the CMA could see a very significant rise in leniency applications. These will consist of parallel filings to those made to the European Commission after Brexit by companies who predominantly operate globally. Multinationals may be more likely to make parallel filings in all major competition law jurisdictions to ensure they benefit from leniency in the event of an investigation. The size of the UK's economy means that the overwhelming majority of multinational antitrust infringements in the EU are likely to affect its markets in some way. While the volume of cartel cases is likely to remain only a fraction of merger cases by number, the CMA's full engagement in this area of enforcement will be significant in securing an important source of revenue for HM Treasury. As Table 1.1 illustrates, almost €30 billion in fines imposed by the European Commission since 1990 have benefited EU Member States, including the UK. It will be important that the CMA continues to impose a level of fines that is commensurate with the impact international cartels have on the UK, both in terms of maintaining the same deterrent effect that is achieved by EU penalties, and in maintaining a significant source of revenue.

In order to be ready for this increase in workload and ensure there is no gap in enforcement that might cause a spike in anti-competitive outcomes, the UK government increased the CMA's budget by £20m, to around £90m per annum, and increased its staff from 640 in March 2018 to 853 a year

Table 1.1 EU cartel fines 1990–2017 (not adjusted for General Court and CJEU judgments)

Year	Amount in euros (€)
1990–1994	537,491,550
1995–1999	292,838,000
2000–2004	3,458,421,100
2005–2009	9,355,867,500
2010–2014	7,917,218,674
2015–2019	8,307,828,000
Total	**29,869,664,824**

Source: European Commission, 'Cartel statistics', http://ec.europa .eu/competition/cartels/statistics/statistics.pdf (accessed 24 August 2020).

later.[41] The issue is not just one of resources, but also of implementing institutional changes to reflect the new demands on procedures, information-gathering and expertise. For example, the significantly enhanced international dimension to the CMA's work could prove very challenging at first in terms of experience and expertise. It is notable that before Brexit there was some criticism of the number and speed of non-merger cases completed by the CMA, as this had been significantly lower than other national competition authorities within the EU.[42] We should be careful about measuring a regulator's success by the number of cases completed, as this does not necessarily equate to deterrence, but a low throughput of cases will undoubtedly make the anticipated increase in enforcement case numbers more challenging. Lyons raises a further issue, which is that the CMA will find it harder to deflect pressure from government departments and from businesses. The European Commission provided some helpful distance, in this respect, between the CMA and the most contentious cases.[43]

It is also worth considering possible implications for regional enforcement within the UK. Whilst the UK is not a federation of states, varying levels of power are devolved to a number of regions and cities. The most notable of these are Scotland, Wales and Northern Ireland, where the regional governments have exclusive competency for health, social services, food safety, education (including universities), agriculture and the environment.[44] Readers not familiar with UK law may be surprised to learn that Scotland and Northern Ireland have distinct legal systems, which is why reference will sometimes be made in this book to the 'Law of England and Wales' and to 'Scots Law'. In May 2014, the CMA announced the opening of regional offices in Edinburgh, Cardiff and Belfast, to 'build a strong centre of intelligence and insight through which the CMA can be more effective in reaching out and responding to the different economic and political dynamics of the devolved nations'.[45] Following the Scottish independence referen-

---

41 See B Lyons, 'Unfinished Reform of the Institutions Enforcing UK competition Law' in B Rodger, P Whelan and A MacCulloch (eds), *The UK Competition Law Regime: A Twenty-Year Retrospective* (Oxford University Press 2021).

42 National Audit Office Report, *The UK Competition Regime* (5 February 2016) HC 737, with reference to a 2010 NAO report that had made similar criticisms of the CMA's predecessor – the Office of Fair Trading.

43 B Lyons, 'Unfinished Reform of the Institutions Enforcing UK Competition Law' in B Rodger, P Whelan and A MacCulloch (eds), *The UK Competition Law Regime: A Twenty Year Retrospective* (Oxford University Press 2021).

44 These were established by the Scotland Act 1998, Wales Act 1998 and the 1998 Belfast Agreement (also known as the Good Friday Agreement) in the case of Northern Ireland.

45 CMA Press Release, 'CMA Announces New Appointments in Scotland, Wales and Northern Ireland' (7 May 2014).

dum later that year, a commission was established to make recommendations for the further devolution of powers to the Scottish Parliament.[46] This included consideration of whether the Scottish government should have some involvement in competition policy or in the decision making of the CMA.[47] It resulted in Scotland Act 2016, s.63, which allows Scottish ministers to ask the CMA (with the consent of the UK government) to undertake a market investigation, in accordance with Enterprise Act 2002, s.139. This is a useful tool where the Scottish government has particular concerns about markets that are local to Scotland that might otherwise escape the attention of the CMA as the UK-wide competition authority.

Brexit has created a number of tensions between the UK government and the devolved administrations. The case could be made for greater delegation of competition powers that would be focused on regional enforcement, leaving the CMA to focus on cases that are truly UK-wide or international in scope. This is something the ruling Scottish government would likely favour as a further precursor to independence. It might also be a sensible way of dealing with the special status of Northern Ireland, which continues to follow some EU rules (including State aid) in order to avoid the need for a hard border with the Republic of Ireland.[48] The problem is that UK markets do not generally divide along these devolved lines. While there may be markets that *mainly* operate within Scotland and Wales, mergers which qualify for review under the Enterprise Act, for example, are often likely to affect trade with the rest of the UK. This is due to the relative size of regions that do not have devolved administrations. For example, Scotland's GDP is lower than that of East Anglia, and the combined GDP of Scotland, Wales and Northern Ireland is less than that of the South East of England, excluding London. Even in more geographically balanced federal economies like Germany, devolved enforcement tends to be limited to local anti-competitive behaviour such as bid-rigging of public procurement contracts.

Finally, Brexit will also have implications for institutions outside the UK. We have already mentioned the impact on the European Commission and the possible need to revise merger regulation turnover thresholds (discussed in more detail in Chapter 4). Brexit could increase the caseload of

---

46 The Smith Commission, *Final Report for Further Devolution of Powers to the Scottish Parliament* (27 November 2014).

47 A Andreangeli, 'Devolution of Competition Policy under the Scotland Act 2016 after Brexit: Straining at the Edges of the Current Settlement?' (2021) 9(1) Journal of Antitrust Enforcement 54–77.

48 Revised Protocol to the Withdrawal Agreement (New Protocol on Ireland/Northern Ireland) (17 October 2019), Article 10. See also Cabinet Office, *The UK's Approach to the Northern Ireland Protocol* (May 2020) CP226, para 40.

national competition authorities of Member States that have high volumes of trade with the UK, such as the Republic of Ireland, Belgium and the Netherlands. Power points out that there are many cases involving Irish markets that were only caught by EU law by virtue of the inclusion of UK turnover or of the effect on trade between the UK and Ireland.[49] There may also therefore be resource and workload implications for these authorities. The possible fragmentation and duplication of workload highlights the importance of continued cooperation between the CMA and other national competition authorities, particularly those within the EU.

1.2.2 Cooperation with EU institutions

While the CMA is already a well-respected competition agency internationally, Brexit requires the authority to reconsider its approach to cooperation with the European Commission and national competition authorities (NCAs) as a third-country agency. It must also strengthen cooperation agreements to assist it in dealing with international casework. Regulation 1/2003 makes legal provision for coordination and sharing of information between the Commission and respective Member State NCAs. The CMA suggested it would be 'very inefficient' if in the future the UK and EU could not share confidential information when investigating the same anti-competitive conduct.[50] This is a reference to the type of information that is freely available to all EU NCAs through the European Competition Network (ECN).[51] Yet the TCA details cooperation in relation to competition enforcement between the European Commission and the CMA in general terms only, and there is no special associate membership of the ECN for the CMA.[52] The language is very similar to other trade agreements, in that each party shall 'endeavour to cooperate and coordinate' in relation to enforcement.[53] Indeed, this reflects the language contained in

---

49 V Power, 'The Implications of Brexit for Competition Law – An Irish Perspective' (2017) 20(1) Irish Journal of European Law 1–15.
50 Written evidence from the Competition and Markets Authority (CMP0002) reported in House of Lords European Union Committee, *Brexit: Competition and State Aid,* 12th Report of Session 2017–19 (2 February 2018) HL Paper 67, para 151.
51 A Andreangeli, 'EU Competition Law Put to the Brexit Test: What Impact Might the Exit of the UK from the Union Have on the Enforcement of the Competition Rules' (2018) 17 Yearbook of Antitrust and Regulatory Studies 7–28, Part 3.
52 TCA Article 2.4 of Title XI. See also European Commission, *Draft Text of the Agreement on the New Partnership with the United Kingdom* (18 March 2020), UKTF (2020) 14, Chapter 2 at 2.16.
53 ibid, Article 2.4(3).

the draft comprehensive free trade agreement published by the UK government in May 2020.[54] Unfortunately, despite the range of different types of competition authority cooperation agreements worldwide, there is no precedent for emulating the level of information exchange facilitated by the ECN, between the competition authorities of two independent jurisdictions.[55] Even the bilateral cooperation agreement between the European Commission and the Swiss Authority for example, which one would expect to be very far-reaching given the close relationship between Switzerland and the EU, has considerable limitations as to both the type of information that can be exchanged and how it can be used.[56]

The exchange of confidential information is curtailed by the protections that exist in domestic law, but more importantly by the impact that exchange might have on enforcement. In the context of merger control, information exchange is more straightforward because it is a consensual process in which all those involved want to achieve a resolution – ideally a merger clearance. It is also an ex ante process whose function, crucially, is not to determine whether there has been an ex post infringement of the law. By contrast, the stakes in antitrust enforcement are very high and competition authorities are particularly guarded about sharing confidential information that may have been gathered through a leniency programme or settlement procedure. Providing wider access to leniency documentation submitted by businesses would potentially undermine these tools, by discouraging firms from coming forward to report cartels or making it less likely that firms will opt for a streamlined procedure that reduces the scope for costly appeals. The exchange of leniency information can occur within the EU's ECN, because the infringement can only be investigated by one EU authority, in a context where leniency applications may have been submitted to multiple authorities, including the Commission. As Wagner-von Papp points out,

> not letting third countries participate in the close cooperation in the ECN is not an arbitrary choice. The close cooperation within the ECN is built on the basis not only of mutual trust and the duty of sincere cooperation under Article 4(3) TEU, but also on the basis of

54 UK Government, *Draft Working Text for a Comprehensive Free Trade Agreement between the United Kingdom and the European Union* (May 2020), Article 22.2.
55 Written evidence of the Centre for Law Economics and Society at UCL (CMP0032) reported in House of Lords European Union Committee, *Brexit: Competition and State Aid,* 12th Report of Session 2017–19 (2 February 2018) HL Paper 67, para 156.
56 Written evidence by Andrea Coscelli, reported in House of Lords European Union Committee, *Brexit: Competition and State Aid*, 12th Report of Session 2017–19 (2 February 2018) HL Paper 67, para 156.

the guarantee of fundamental rights under Article 6(3) TEU and the Charter on Fundamental Rights, as well as on the basis of adjudication of any arising issues by the CJEU as the ultimate arbiter of EU law.[57]

Moreover, sharing confidential information between independent jurisdictions increases the likelihood of multiple investigations and higher fines, as well as the possible prospect of criminal prosecutions. For these reasons, the continued exchange of confidential information between the CMA and the European Commission may be very limited.

The CMA can expect a level of cooperation with its EU counterparts that is more typical of bilateral arrangements between competition authorities of independent jurisdictions. These arrangements typically facilitate the exchange of some confidential information, but with serious limits to how it can be used. For example, in September 2020 the CMA signed a Multilateral Mutual Assistance and Cooperation Framework for Competition Authorities (MMAC) with its counterparts in Australia, Canada, New Zealand and the United States.[58] The agreement is ambitious in that it facilitates cooperation in investigating and gathering evidence to reflect the increasingly international nature of competition cases. However, confidential information can only be shared to the extent allowed by domestic law (which typically requires the consent of the firm being investigated) and with the permission of the authority providing it as to its use.[59] This means that agreements like the MMAC have in the past been principally effective at coordinating merger regulation and antitrust enforcement, only where the firm is cooperating with authorities in both jurisdictions.[60]

While the value of any cooperation must not be underestimated (especially in reducing the scope for diverging merger decisions),[61] the inferior levels of potential exchange of information between the CMA and its European counterparts in the ECN will compound the duplication of work and the time and resources needed to complete investigations, both in the

---

57 F Wagner-von Papp, 'Competition Law in EU Free Trade and Cooperation Agreements (and What the UK Can Expect after Brexit)' (2017) European Yearbook of International Economic Law 2017, 301–359 at 352–353.

58 CMA Press Release, 'CMA to Increase Competition Cooperation with International Partners' (2 September 2020).

59 See, for example, MM Dabbah, *International and Comparative Competition Law* (Cambridge University Press 2010), 517.

60 F Jenny, 'International Cooperation on Competition: Myth, Reality and Perspective' (2003) The Antitrust Bulletin 973.

61 JJ Parisi, 'Cooperation Among Competition Authorities in Merger Regulation' (2010) Cornell International Law Journal 42–69.

UK and the EU. This will be especially challenging given the scale and complexity of undertaking investigations into international cartel agreements, the meetings for which may have occurred entirely outside the jurisdiction of the UK.[62] Demetriou points out that by virtue of procedural variances that exist between EU and UK law, there are already important differences in the standard of review and treatment of evidence. She suggests that the CMA's enhanced workload could be made all the more difficult by the fact challenges to its decisions will be 'lengthier, costlier and involve a more intensive review and focus on evidence'.[63]

1.3 Concluding remarks on institutions and cooperation

We have seen how the real challenges of Brexit for competition law and policy in the UK did not lie in the design of the UK's enforcement regime, or require any significant changes to UK substantive competition law rules. With the exception of the contentious issue of State aid, the UK's competition regime was reasonably well placed to transition from that of an EU Member State to an independent third country. The most immediate challenges related to the CMA's ability to scale up its enforcement and ensure that UK markets and consumers are no less protected than they were previously within the EU. The period of adjustment and transition could expose particular vulnerabilities in terms of delays and the CMA will need to manage resource pressures carefully, and thereby ensure that any spike in merger clearance work, for example, does not necessitate a short-term weakening in the enforcement of the antitrust rules. The focus will very much be on the CMA to meet these challenges and perform better than it has ever done in the past. We revisit aspects of these institutional challenges throughout the rest of this book, which is focused on the practical implications of having UK and EU competition laws operating in parallel, beginning with consideration of the impact of Brexit on antitrust rules.

---

62 P Roth, 'Competition Law and Brexit: The Challenges Ahead' (2017) 43(1) Competition Law Journal 5, at 7.
63 M Demetriou, 'The Future Is a Foreign Country: They Do Things Differently There – The Impact of Brexit on the Enforcement of Competition Law' (2018) 39(3) European Competition Law Review 99. See also A Psygkas, 'The "Double Helix" of Process and Substance Review before the UK Competition Appeal Tribunal: A Model Case or a Cautionary Tale for Specialist Courts?' in S Rose-Ackerman and PL Linseth (eds), *Comparative Administrative Law*, 2nd ed (Edward Elgar 2017) 462–477; and A Outhuijse, 'Effective Public Enforcement of Cartels: Rates of Challenged and Annulled Cartel Fines in Ten European Member States' (2019) 42(2) World Competition 171–204.

2 Anti-competitive agreements and abuse of dominance

The fact the substantive antitrust rules of the UK and the EU are materially the same ensures legal certainty in the immediate future and has allowed the UK to transition to a non-EU Member State without the need to make major amendments to legislation. However, the wording of the Articles 101 and 102 prohibitions themselves are not particularly helpful in maintaining legal certainty – in terms of the interpretation and application of the equivalent rules in Competition Act Chapter I and II prohibitions. Indeed, the meaning of terms like 'undertaking', 'concerted practice', 'effect', and 'abuse' are deliberately wide so as to capture a whole spectrum of anti-competitive conduct and adapt to new situations over time. As Roth points out, the core antitrust prohibitions are 'drafted in very broad, open-textured language' and 'there has been no legislative amendment or elaboration of the core text since the original Treaty of Rome was adopted'.[1] This is especially so given that EU competition law case-law makes no reference to the *travaux préparatoires* or legislative intent of the provisions.[2]

Accordingly, for legal certainty in determining the boundaries of antitrust rules, in both the EU and UK, we rely very heavily on block exemption regulations (i.e. safe harbours from liability where certain criteria such as market share thresholds are met), soft law (e.g. guidance published by the competition authority), the decisional practice of the European Commission, and the jurisprudence of the courts. This means that while the wording of the EU and UK prohibitions are likely to remain aligned, their application will inevitably begin to diverge to some extent by virtue of the fact the UK is no longer bound by EU law. Indeed, the wording of the core antitrust prohibitions aimed at anti-competitive agreements and the exercise of unilateral market

---

1 P Roth, 'The Continual Evolution of Competition Law' (2019) 7 Journal of Antitrust Enforcement 6–26 at 8–10.
2 ibid, 10.

DOI: 10.4324/9781351105446-2

power are very similar across a whole range of non-EU legal jurisdictions, yet there are significant differences in their precise scope and application.

The purpose of this chapter is to analyse the interpretation and application of these antitrust rules, with a focus on the substantive rules rather than procedure. We begin by looking at the status of EU law before and after Brexit. We then identify the most contentious areas of Article 101 and 102, where divergence in the interpretation and application of the UK prohibitions may be anticipated in the medium and long term. There follows a discussion of sanctions against individuals involved in cartels, and consideration of the particular challenges posed by competition policy in relation to the environment.

2.1 The status of EU law after Brexit

In order to ensure legal certainty, the European Union (Withdrawal) Act 2018, s.6 provides that UK courts continue to be bound by EU case law that is delivered before the end of the implementation period (IP completion day, previously referred to as 'exit day') and relates to *retained* EU law. S.6(4) provides that the Supreme Court of the United Kingdom[3] can depart from any retained EU case law, applying the same test as it would in deciding whether to depart from its own precedent – namely 'whether it appears right to do so'.[4] Following a consultation in late 2020, the government noted the dangers of departing from existing EU case law, but considered it appropriate to extend the power to do so to certain courts, notably the Court of Appeal of England and Wales, the Court of Appeal of Northern Ireland and the Inner House of the Court of Session in Scotland.[5] The test to be applied by the courts is no stricter than that of the Supreme Court. The rationale for extension of the power to depart to lower courts focused on concerns about increased workload and delays for the Supreme Court, and risks that the scope to evolve and depart from retained EU case law – where it was genuinely right to do so – would be unnecessarily constrained.

The freedom to depart from EU precedent was extended to the interpretation of the domestic prohibitions by The Competition (Amendment etc.) (EU Exit) Regulations. It replaced the Competition Act 1998, s.60 (the requirement of equivalence with EU law) with 's.60A – Certain principles etc to be considered or applied from IP completion day'. This requires the

---

3 This extended to Scotland's High Court of Judiciary in specified cases.

4 House of Lords Practice Statement of 26 July 1966.

5 Ministry of Justice, *Government Response to the Consultation on the Departure from Retained EU Case Law by UK Courts and Tribunals* (October 2020) CP 303.

Competition and Markets Authority (CMA) and UK courts and tribunals to ensure there be no inconsistency between

> 'the principles that it applies, and the decision that it reaches' and 'the principles laid down by the TFEU and the European Court before IP completion day, and any relevant decision made by that Court before IP completion day ... in determining any corresponding question arising in EU law.' (s.60A (2))

They must also have regard to any relevant decision or statement of the European Commission made before IP completion day, unless withdrawn. This obligation does not exist where the principle is excluded by the regulation (for example in relation to aspects of Article 101 that relate to trade between Member States). However, further exclusions on this obligation are set out in s.60A(7), where the authority or court 'thinks that it is appropriate to act otherwise in light of one or more of the following':

(a) differences between the provisions of this Part under consideration and the corresponding provisions of EU law as those provisions of EU law had effect immediately before IP completion day;
(b) differences between markets in the United Kingdom and markets in the European Union;
(c) developments in forms of economic activity since the time when the principle or decision referred to in subsection (2)(b) was laid down or made;
(d) generally accepted principles of competition analysis or the generally accepted application of such principles;
(e) a principle laid down, or decision made, by the European Court on or after IP completion day;
(f) the particular circumstances under consideration.

This amendment to the Competition Act is intended to balance the need for legal certainty with ensuring that UK authorities and courts have the freedom to develop their own jurisprudence, according to the particular interests of UK markets and consumers. As we shall discuss later, divergence is more likely in cases dealing with new and novel circumstances. These can arise commonly in antitrust, exemplified by the rise of new and fast-changing digital markets, which have recently been the subject of numerous studies and reports at the UK, EU and international level,[6] and subject to wide-

---

6 See in particular 'The Furman Report' – HM Treasury, Unlocking digital competition, Report of the Digital Competition Expert Panel (13 March 2019).

ranging challenges worldwide, including by the European Commission. However, it should be noted that UK judges are generally very reluctant to overturn clear precedent, for reasons of legal certainty and for fear that they are seen to erode the separation of powers between the judiciary and Parliament.[7]

In terms of post-Brexit EU case law, s.60A(8) makes clear that the obligation created by s.60A(2) does not extend to principles laid down or decisions made by the European court after IP completion day (i.e. from 1 January 2021). There was some suggestion that it would be in the UK's interest to create a positive obligation on courts to *have regard to* EU law and precedent[8], but this was not politically acceptable given the imperative to regain sovereignty. Neither would it necessarily have been in the UK's interests to retain such ties with EU law without any influence over its future direction. Instead, post-Brexit EU case law is likely to be *strongly persuasive* for some time and there is every reason to expect the CMA and Competition Appeal Tribunal (CAT) to adopt the same reasoning as future EU cases.[9] Indeed, EU competition law is already very influential for the laws of many non-EU countries around the world.[10] Moreover, the persuasive and instructive nature of legal reasoning from other jurisdictions is not something that is alien to UK courts, which occasionally adopt a precedent from the judgments of other common law jurisdictions, even though there is no obligation to do so.[11] On the other hand, even before Brexit there were instances of the CAT interpreting competition law in a manner that was contradicted by later EU case law.[12] The sequencing of cases may become very significant

---

7 For a definitive study of precedent in English law, see N Duxbury, *The Nature and Authority of Precedent* (Cambridge University Press 2009).

8 See, for example, J Fingleton et al., 'The Implications of Brexit for UK Competition Law and Policy' (2017) 13(3) Journal of Competition Law and Economics 389–422 at 395.

9 Unless the UK is required to implement some EU rules (such as State aid) as part of a free trade agreement, there is no basis in international law for CJEU case law to be given any kind of special status.

10 EU competition law jurisprudence guides judicial decision-making around the world because so many competition prohibitions are based on those of the EU. See, for example, Erdem Büyüksagis, 'The Impact of EU Law on Swiss and Turkish Regulation of Competition – With Specific Consideration Given to Abuse of Dominant Position Cases' in Franz Werro, Başak Baysal and Lukas Heckendorn Urscheler (eds) *L'influence du droit européen en Turquie et en Suisse* (Schulthess 2015), available at http://papers.ssrn.com/so l3/papers.cfm?abstract_id=2579698 (accessed 8 March 2017).

11 For example, *Chester v Afshar* [2004] UKHL 41, which followed the Australian High Court decision in *Chappel v Hart* (1998) 195 CLR 232. See Neil Duxbury, 'The Law of the Land' (2015) 78(1) Modern Law Review 26.

12 Ian McDonald, Warsha Kalé and James Harrison, 'Potential EU-UK Competition Law Divergence Post-Brexit Highlighted by Conflicting Approaches of UK Competition Appeal

in this respect. If the CAT deals with a particular question of law first, it will be unlikely to later amend its approach if a subsequent CJEU case decides differently. The prospects of the Court of Justice of the European Union (CJEU) being persuaded by the reasoning of the CAT are probably more limited. Beyond this, it is highly unlikely that the UK government would consider abandoning or significantly changing the existing UK competition rules, as the voices calling for a softening of law in this area have been very limited.[13] Neither is it immediately obvious that there would be any strong lobbying for them to do so. It is notable that in a survey of small businesses in 2017, for example, competition law was one of the lowest concerns when businesses were asked to identify regulations that provided the greatest barriers.[14] Maintaining these core prohibitions makes it easier for businesses to operate in the UK and the EU (even if there is some divergence over time) and can be of great significance to new free trade agreements forged by the UK. Competition law is not captured by World Trade Organization (WTO) rules and so commitments to tackle anti-competitive behaviour tend to be detailed in trade agreements. However, such provisions are typically unenforceable and therefore more of symbolic value, or simply serve to encourage cooperation between the signatories' competition authorities.[15]

We now turn our focus to the points of law that are most likely to lead to diverging approaches between the two jurisdictions. A detailed and exhaustive analysis of all aspects of Articles 101 and 102 are considered in fuller depth in a range of more comprehensive completion law texts.[16] For the purposes of this book, we simply give a critical overview of the more contentious issues that may drive future divergence.

Tribunal in Recent Pharma Cases' (14 August 2018), Mayer Brown LLP, discussing *Pfizer Inc. and Pfizer Limited v Competition and Markets Authority* [2018] CAT 11. Also contrast, for example, *BetterCare Group Ltd v DGFT* [2002] CAT 7 (Case No 1006/2/1/01) with Case C-205/03 *FENIN*. Judgement of the Court (Grand Chamber) of 11 July 2006.

13 See, for example, a briefing by the British Medical Association calling for competition law and procurement rules to be suspended from healthcare in the UK: BMA, *Brexit Briefing: Competition and Procurement in the Healthcare System* (2017).

14 FSB, *Regulation Returned: What Small Firms Want from Brexit* (July 2017), FSB Brexit Research Series, p. 32.

15 Note, for instance, the first competition policy chapter of a Preferential Trade Agreement in NAFTA: DD Sokol, 'Order without (Enforceable) Law: Why Countries Enter into Non-Enforceable Competition Policy Chapters in Free Trade Agreements' (2008) 83 Chicago-Kent Law Review 270.

16 See in particular R Whish and D Bailey, *Competition Law*, 9th edn (Oxford University Press 2018); A Jones, B Sufrin and N Dunne, *EU Competition Law: Text, Cases and Materials,* 7th edn (Oxford University Press 2019); and A Ezrachi, *EU Competition Law: An Analytical Guide to the Leading Cases,* 6th edn (Hart Publishing 2018).

2.2 Areas of possible divergence under Article 101 TFEU

Article 101 of the Treaty on the Functioning of the European Union (TFEU) and Chapter I of the Competition Act 1998 prohibit anti-competitive agreements, concerted practices (exchanges of information that fall short of an agreement) and decisions of associations of undertakings. They apply to both horizontal and vertical arrangements, meaning that they regulate behaviour between firms, whether they are at the same level of production ('horizontal' – e.g. two manufacturers or retailers) or at different levels ('vertical' – e.g. an agreement between a manufacturer and a retailer). They can also capture complicated arrangements that have elements of both – so-called 'hub and spoke' agreements.[17] Due to the very wide application of Article 101 TFEU, the EU has block exemptions that provide safe harbours for categories of behaviour and particular industries where anti-competitive effects are considered unlikely, or other benefits are likely to outweigh any competition restrictions. The most significant are the general block exemptions on vertical agreements[18] and on horizontal cooperation agreements,[19] as well as more specialist block exemptions on categories of research and development agreements,[20] specialisation agreements[21] and licensing agreements for the transfer of technology.[22] The general vertical block exemption, for example, provides a safe harbour for all vertical agreements (also referred to as 'restraints') apart from a limited number of black-listed clauses, so long as the relevant competitors fall within certain market share thresholds which act as a proxy for the level of risk to competition.

17 See O Odudu, 'Hub and Spoke Collusion' in I Loanos and D Geradin (eds), *Handbook on European Competition Law* (Edward Elgar 2013) Chapter 6; and PA Perinetto, 'Hub-and-Spoke Arrangements: Future Challenges within Article 101 TFEY Assessment' (2019) 15(2–3) European Competition Journal 281–317.

18 Commission Regulation 330/2010 of 20 April 2010 on the application of Article 101(3) of the Treaty on the Functioning of the European Union to categories of vertical agreements and concerted practices [2010} OJ L 102.

19 Council Regulation No 281/71 on application of Article 85(3) [now 101(3)] of the Treaty to categories of agreements, decisions and concerted practices [1971] OJ L 285.

20 Commission Regulation No 1217/2010 of 14 December 2010 on the application of Article 101(3) of the Treaty of the functioning of the European Union to categories of research and development agreements [2010] OJ L 335.

21 Commission Regulation No 1218/2010 of 14 December 2010 on the application of Article 101(3) of the Treaty to categories of specialization agreements [2010] OJ L 335.

22 Commission Regulation (EU) No 316/2014 of 21 March 2014 on the application of Article 101(3) of the Treaty on the Functioning of the European Union to categories of technology transfer agreements [2014] OJ L 93.

The areas at high risk of divergence between Article 101 TFEU and Chapter I of the Competition Act 1998 include the following.

Diverging block exemptions – The EU block exemptions detailed earlier have been adopted into UK law by statutory instrument, to apply in relation to agreements potentially caught by the Chapter I prohibition, but are time-limited and have their current expiry dates preserved.[23] Most are due to expire in 2022, which means that any divergence in the scope of these safe harbours could occur very swiftly, unless both jurisdictions choose to renew them in largely the same form. This creates some uncertainty for businesses that are planning future vertical distribution arrangements and joint ventures with competitors in the UK and the EU. It is in the UK's interests to keep block exemptions broadly aligned for the benefit of these businesses. For example, less generous block exemptions in the UK could cause some EU firms to stop trading there altogether. There would also be little benefit in making the exemptions significantly more generous, as this could make UK consumers more vulnerable to agreements that could potentially reduce competition.

The boundary between 'Object' and 'Effect' – Behaviour caught by Article 101 is prohibited if it has either the 'object' or 'effect' of restricting competition. Conduct falling into the first category is considered the most serious form of anti-competitive agreement, and accordingly is treated as unlawful regardless of its effects or whether it was properly implemented. Where conduct does not have the object of restricting competition, its effects must be considered in their full economic context.[24] Effects cases are unpredictable and involve costly detailed analysis of the market, and so it has been suggested that the European Commission has been slowly expanding the boundaries of 'object' category agreements, because they make for administratively easier infringement decisions.[25] The question that has arisen before the CJEU is what factors need to be present for an agreement to be considered as 'by object' and when some kind of abridged effects analysis is necessary in making this calculation.[26] There is sizeable literature on this issue and a very lively academic debate as to the correct criteria that

---

23 The Competition (Amendment etc.) (EU Exit) Regulations 2019, Part 2.
24 Case 56/65 *STM* [1966] 1 CMLR 357 at 375 and Case T-374/94 *European Night Services* [1999] ECR II-3141 at 136.
25 See, for example, A Stephan and M Hviid, 'Cover Pricing and the Overreach of "Object" Liability under Article 101 TFEU' (2015) 38(4) World Competition 507.
26 Contrast Case C-8/08, *T-Mobile Netherlands BV v. Raad van bestuur van de Nederlandse Mededingingsautoriteit* with Case C-67/13 P, *Groupemont des cartes bancaires (CB) v. European Commission*, 11 September 2014 and subsequent case law, for example.

should be applied.[27] Until its infringement decision in ComparetheMarket. com in November 2020, the CMA (and Office of Fair Trading [OFT] before it) had never made an infringement decision solely on the basis that the conduct had the 'effect' of distorting competition under either provision.[28] The immediate priority of keeping pace with international 'object' cases and the costly time and resource implications of establishing an effects infringement make it unlikely they will prioritise enforcement resources on effects cases. However, the fact there is limited UK decisional practice on this issue, combined with the new s.60A, could allow the UK to take an entirely novel approach to this question when it arises.

The inconsistent application of Article 101(3) – This is often referred to as the 'efficiency defence' to anti-competitive agreements and has expression in the Competition Act 1998, s.9(1). In the absence of benefiting from a relevant block exemption, an agreement can both escape liability under Article 101(1) and be enforceable in court against contracting parties where any restriction of competition is outweighed by resulting efficiency gains. This is the case where the agreement: improves the production or distribution of goods or promotes technical or economic progress; and allows consumers a fair share of the benefits; and does not contain dispensable restrictions (i.e. the same outcome cannot be achieved by other means); and must not substantially eliminate competition in the market. The application of these criteria is subjective to some extent, and it is notable that the EU case law on the third and fourth criterion is quite limited. Importantly, this efficiency defence can in principle apply to all infringements of Article 101 or Chapter I, although it is considered very unlikely to succeed in relation to hard-core cartel conduct.[29]

---

27 See in particular A Jones, 'The Journey toward an Effects-Based Approach under Article 101 TFEU – The Case of Hardcore Restraints' (2010) 55(4) The Antitrust Bulletin 783–818; O Odudu, 'Restrictions of Competition by Object – What's the Beef?' (2008) 8 Competition Law Journal 11; O Odudu, *The Boundaries of EC Competition Law: The Scope of Article 81* (Oxford University Press 2006) 61; D Bailey, 'Restrictions of Competition by Object Under Article 101 TFEU' (2012) 49 Common Market Law Review 559–600 at 563–564; R Nazzini and A Nikpay, 'Object Restriction and Two-Sided Markets in EU Competition Law after Cartes Bancaires' (2014) 10(2) Competition Policy International 157–172; J Killick and J Jourdan, *'Cartes Bancaires*: A Revolution or a Reminder of Old Principles We Should Never Have Forgotten?' (2014) Competition Policy International 14–3.

28 B Rodger, 'Application of the Domestic and EU Antitrust Prohibitions: An Analysis of the UK Competition Authority's Enforcement Practice' (2020) 8(1) Journal of Antitrust Enforcement 86–123; Decision of the Competition and Markets Authority – Price comparison website: use of most favoured nation clauses. case 50505. 19 November 2020. See also: A Jones, 'Vertical Agreements' ch 3 in B Rodger, P Whelan and A MacCulloch (Eds), The UK Competition Regime, A Twenty-Year Retrospective (OUP, 2021).

29 Commission Notice – Guidelines on the application of Article 81(3) of the Treaty [2004] OJ C 101, para 46.

The central issue under Article 101(3) has been the extent to which courts may take into consideration factors that go beyond economic efficiency. The uncertainty that surrounded this was of limited importance while the European Commission enjoyed the exclusive competence to apply it under the notification procedure that existed under the old Regulation 17/62, between 1962 and 2004. During this period there were examples where, in applying Article 101(3), the Commission and the courts appeared to be influenced by non-efficiency factors, such as stabilising employment and creating jobs in a poor region of the European Economic Community.[30] When Regulation 1/2003 was introduced, national competition authorities (NCAs) and national courts could apply Article 101 in full for the first time, and the European Commission's 2004 guidance on Article 101(3) focused on a narrow efficiency-based approach.[31] Despite this and other efforts to ensure consistency (e.g. through the European Competition Network [ECN]), there is some evidence of diverging approaches between EU Member States in how non-competition factors appear to be taken into account, albeit under the guise of one of the four criteria set out in 101(3) itself.[32] The long-standing uncertainties surrounding the scope of Article 101(3) make it susceptible to use as a back door to exempting anti-competitive agreements on wider policy grounds. For example, environmental protection (discussed later) and industrial policy could both create pressures on competition authorities and the courts, especially in light of s.60A in the UK.

The treatment of resale price maintenance (RPM) – Any agreement that includes a provision preventing a retailer from charging less than a minimum price falls under the 'object' category and is blacklisted under the vertical block exemption regulation.[33] Although EU law treats minimum RPM as being

---

30 See Case 26/76, *Metro v Commission* [1977] 2 CMLR 1; and *Ford / Volkswagen* [1993] 5 CMLR 617. See discussion in G Monti, 'Article 81 EC and Public Policy' (2002) 39 Common Market Law Review 1057–1099; B Sufrin, 'The Evolution of Article 81(3) of the EC Treaty' (2006) 51(4) The Antitrust Bulletin 915; CD Ehlermann, 'The Modernization of EC Antitrust Policy: A Legal and Cultural Revolution' (2000) 37 Common Market Law Review 537–590.

31 Guidelines on the application of Article 81(3) of the Treaty (2004/C 101/08); O Odudu (n 27) Chapter 7; C Townley, 'Which Goals Count in Article 101 TFEU?: Public Policy and Its Discontents' (2011) 9 European Competition Law Review 441; R Wesseling, 'The Draft-Regulation Modernising the Competition Rules: The Commission Is Married to One Idea' (2001) 26(4) European Law Review 357.

32 See O Brook, 'Struggling with Article 101(3) TFEU: Diverging Approaches of the Commission, EU Courts, and Five Competition Authorities' (2019) 56(1) Common Market Law Review 121–156.

33 Commission Regulation (EU) No 330/2010 of 20 April 2010 on the application of Article 101(3) of the Treaty on the Functioning of the European Union to categories of vertical

among the most serious infringements of competition law, the economics of this practice indicate that RPM's beneficial or harmful effects may depend on the particular characteristics of the market.[34] The EU approach contrasts with the treatment of minimum RPM in the US since the Supreme Court case of *Leegin*, which categorised resale price maintenance mechanisms as subject to the rule of reason (i.e. only unlawful where there is a net anti-competitive effect, instead of being per se illegal).[35] In particular, minimum RPM can help overcome the *free rider* problem and incentivise distributors and retailers to promote and successfully launch new products, despite frustrating *intrabrand* competition between retailers.[36] The UK may therefore decide to treat minimum RPM more permissively or to take a more nuanced approach to its regulation, for example through some kind of shorthand effects analysis. Given the CMA's continued prioritisation of enforcement against RPM practices, any potential divergence here is unlikely in the short term.[37]

2.3 Areas of possible divergence under Article 102 TFEU

The law on abuse of dominance provides even greater scope for divergence because it covers more types of behaviour and has been subject to a body of case law that might best be described as comparatively sparse, contradictory and still very much developing. Moreover, whereas there is general universal consensus on the opprobrium to be attached to hard-core anti-competitive agreements that lie at the vanguard of the Commission and CMA's Article 101 and Chapter I enforcement activities, there is considerably wider academic debate and disagreement about the appropriate scope of and range of conduct to be prohibited by an anti-competitive rule aimed at abusive unilateral conduct.[38] The US and EU take very different

agreements and concerted practices [2010] OJ L 102, Article 4(a).
34 See M Bennett et al., 'Resale Price Maintenance: Explaining the Controversy, and Small Steps Towards a More Nuanced Policy' (2011) 33(4) Fordham International Law Journal 1278–1299.
35 *Leegin Creative Leather Products, Inc. v. PSKS, Inc.* (2007) 127 S. Ct. 2705.
36 A Jones, 'Completion of the Revolution in Antitrust Doctrine on Restricted Distribution: *Leegin* and Its Implications for EC Competition Law' (2008) 53(4) Antitrust Bulletin 903; and A Jones, 'Brexit: Implications for UK Competition Law' (2017) King's College London Dickson Poon School of Law, Legal Studies Research Paper Series: Paper No 2017-21, p. 12.
37 B Rodger, 'Application of the Domestic and EU Antitrust Prohibitions: An Analysis of the UK Competition Authority's Enforcement Practice' (2020) 8(1) Journal of Antitrust Enforcement 86–123.
38 See generally, LL Gormsen, *A Principled Approach to Abuse of Dominance in European Competition Law* (Cambridge University Press 2010); P Akman, *The Concept of Abuse in EU Competition Law* (Hart Publishing 2012).

approaches to this area of law, for example, the former being far more cautious to interfere with monopoly power that has been gained as the 'reward' of being successful in the market.[39]

In this context, it is important to note that Article 102 only applies to dominant firms (i.e. those with a market share of around 40% or more) and that abuse of dominance cases and infringement findings by the UK competition authorities have been rare.[40] Indeed, the UK abuse of dominance prohibition has been more significant in private actions seeking injunctive relief – usually in the form of access to an essential facility, or in dealing with a refusal to supply.[41] The categories of conduct Article 102 and Chapter II apply to include:

1. Excessive pricing – using monopoly power (for example in relation to a product protected by a patent) to engage in price gouging, or otherwise charging a price that is not considered reasonable or fair.
2. Predatory pricing – deliberately setting prices low (typically at a loss) for a period in order to drive a competitor out of the market or deter a prospective new entrant.
3. Loyalty discounts and rebates – using rebates linked to quantity or loyalty to ensure there is no benefit for customers to buy from a competitor.
4. Tying – leveraging monopoly power in one market to restrict competition in a second, closely related market (e.g. nail guns and nails, as in *Hilti*).[42]
5. Refusal to deal/essential facilities – using control over an 'essential facility' to eliminate competition by refusing to supply to a downstream competitor (e.g. the owner of a port only allowing access to its own ferries, as in *Sealink/B&I Holyhead*).[43]

The areas at high risk of divergence between Article 102 TFEU and Chapter II of the Competition Act 1998, include the following:

A more economic approach – The Commission's 2009 guidance on Article 102 was meant to signal a move away from a form-based ordoliberal

---

39 See RE Bloch, H-G Kamann, JS Brown, and JP Schmidt 'A Comparative Analysis of Article 82 and Section 2 of the Sherman Act' (2006) 7 Business Law International 136.
40 See, for example, B Rodger, 'Application of the Domestic and EU Antitrust Prohibitions: An Analysis of the UK Competition Authority's Enforcement Practice' (2020) 8(1) Journal of Antitrust Enforcement 86–123.
41 For example *Purple Parking Ltd & Ancor v Heathrow Airport* [2011] EWHC 987 (Ch).
42 C-53/92 ECR 1994/3/I-667.
43 [1992] 5 CMLR 255.

approach to abuse of dominance to one that was more effects-based.[44] This meant that rather than applying per se prohibitions to categories of exclusionary behaviour, there would be an assessment of its measurable effects on the market. This was considered important to distinguish competition on the merits (which has beneficial effects for consumers and should be promoted) from conduct that is likely to result in foreclosure and harm to consumers. Subsequent case law has reflected a tension between effects and formalist approaches to abuse of dominance, most notably in the *Intel* case in relation to rebates.[45] The Commission found that Intel had abused its dominant position in the context of exclusivity rebates and held that those rebates could be categorised as abusive, without any analysis of the particular circumstances of the case or the effects on the market.[46] This was upheld by the General Court,[47] but then rejected by the CJEU, which found that it was wrong to treat loyalty rebates as per se illegal and that it was incumbent on the Commission to show that a specific rebates arrangement is capable of restricting competition, as part of any infringement decision.[48] In particular, they must apply the 'as-efficient-competitor test' (determining whether the conduct is capable of excluding a competitor which is as efficient as the dominant firm). The judgment means that a more thorough analysis is required when the dominant firm submits evidence that its exclusive arrangements are not capable of restricting competition.[49] There is still some debate as to which approach is more desirable[50] and the UK's approach to this question could end up being quite different by virtue of s.60A.[51] The dearth of any purely effects Chapter I

---

44 European Commission, *Guidance on Enforcement Priorities in Applying Article 102 to Exclusionary Conduct by Dominant Undertakings* [2009] C45/7; see Pinar Akman, 'The European Commission's Guidance on Article 102 TFEU: From *Inferno* to *Paradiso*?' (2010) 73(4) Modern Law Review 605; John Vickers, 'Abuse of Market Power' (2005) 115(504) The Economic Journal 244.

45 Judgement of 12 June 2014 in Case T-286/09 *Intel v European Commission*.

46 Commission Decision of 13 May 2009, *Intel* COMP/C-2/37.990.

47 General Court Judgement of 12 June 2014, *Intel v Commission*, ECLI:EU:T:2014:547.

48 Case-413/14 *Intel v European Commission* P EU:C:2017:632;

49 A Jones, 'Brexit: Implications for UK Competition Law' (2017), King's College London Dickson Poon School of Law, Legal Studies Research Paper Series: Paper No 2017-21, p. 12.

50 For example, contrast the views of W Wils, 'The Judgement of the EU General Court in Intel and the So-Called More Economic Approach to Abuse of Dominance' (2014) 37(4) World Competition 405–434; with P Rey, 'An Effects-Based Approach to Article 102: A Response to Wouter Wils' (2015) 38(1) World Competition 3–29.

51 In any event, note the CAT's ruling that it was not appropriate to apply the AEC test in *Royal Mail v OFCOM* [2019] CAT 27.

infringement cases in the UK and the low number of abuse cases, more generally, may not bode well for a more economics-based approach to the enforcement of Chapter II.

What is a fair price? – The test set out in *United Brands* for excessive pricing is 'whether the difference between the costs actually incurred and the price actually charged is excessive' and if so 'whether the price has been imposed which is either unfair in itself or when compared to competing products'.[52] This area of abuse of dominance is essentially meant to deal with price gouging–type behaviour. However, the question of what constitutes an excessive price is highly subjective. Many competition authorities are wary of using competition law to directly control prices in the market, especially as it amounts to a behavioural remedy that requires some ex-post monitoring. The complexities of excessive pricing cases are illustrated by the CMA's case against Flynn Pharma, in which the cost to the NHS of an anti-epilepsy drug increased from £2m in 2012 to £50m in 2013. Flynn successfully challenged the decision before the CAT, in a judgment that was largely upheld by the Court of Appeal. They found that the CMA had misapplied *United Brands*, failed to ascertain a hypothetical benchmark price and failed to adequately evaluate comparable products.[53] The challenge before the Court of Appeal demonstrated a disagreement between the CMA and the CAT as to the correct application of EU law on this issue.

Recoupment and predatory pricing – EU competition law takes a particularly restrictive approach to predatory pricing. In essence, under the test set out in *Akzo*,[54] when businesses price below their average variable cost (AVC)[55] there is an assumption of anti-competitive intent or a plan to foreclose a competitor, and even prices above AVC can be an abuse if there is evidence of such a plan.[56] This contrasts with the approach in the US under *Brooke Group*, in which s.2 of the Sherman Act (the US equivalent of Article 102) is only breached if the price is below the

---

52 *United Brands*, para 252.

53 *Phlynn Pharma Ltd v CMA* [2018] CAT 11; *Competition and Markets Authority v Flynn Pharma Ltd* [2020] EWCA Civ 617.

54 C 62/86 *Akzo Chemie BV v Commission*, ECLI:EU:C:1991:286.

55 Taken as a proxy of marginal cost, which is harder to measure.

56 Abuse of dominance is generally focused on the objective form of the conduct, but here the Commission will consider internal documents and communications that suggest a predatory strategy or intent. See C O'Grady, 'The Role of Exclusionary Intent in the Enforcement of Article 102 TFEU' (2014) 37(4) World Competition 459–486.

AVC and it can be shown that the firm is able to later recoup its losses.[57] This is thought to be key to confirming that low pricing is indeed predatory and not competitive, thereby ensuring an effects-based approach. The CAT has followed the EU approach but may be influenced in the future by the considerable academic and economic debate on the merits of this issue, especially on whether an abuse should exist where it is not possible to demonstrate the recoupment of losses.[58]

Dynamic efficiency and property rights – One of the more controversial questions in abuse of dominance is the extent to which competition law should interfere with the property rights of dominant firms – whether by requiring them to give competitors access to a physical essential facility, as in *Sealink/B&I-Holyhead*, or to license intellectual property, as in *Magill*.[59] However, both of these cases involved exceptional circumstances that meant there could be no competition without forcing the firms to give access to their competitors. For example, in *Magill* it was impossible to fulfil an important consumer demand (a TV guide containing information on all the channels) without this access. Rather, the controversy was left by the European Commission's 2004 *Microsoft* case, which forced the firm to share its interoperability codes (which were protected by intellectual property rights) with competitors in order to facilitate competition for software that was compatible with the Microsoft Windows Operating System.[60] The General Court rejected an appeal from Microsoft and drew considerable criticism for appearing to ignore how the Commission's decision failed to demonstrate the codes were necessary for a resulting 'new product', despite this being central to the exceptional circumstances that justified the intervention in cases like *Magill*.[61]

The CMA has not engaged in cases that require businesses to share their intellectual property, but the *Microsoft* case casts a long shadow

---

57 509 U.S. 209 (1993); L Kaplow, 'Recoupment, Market Power and Predatory Pricing' (2018–2019) 82 Antitrust Law Journal 167.

58 See, for example, R O'Donoghue and J Padilla, *The Law and Economics of Article 102 TFEU* (Hart 2014), at 6.4.1; and KG Elzinga and DE Mills, 'Predatory Pricing' in RD Blair and DD Sokol (eds), *The Oxford Handbook of International Antitrust Economics*, Volume 2 (Oxford University Press 2015) Chapter 2.

59 Cases C- 241/91, *P etc RTE and ITP v Commission* [1995] ECR I- 743, [1995] 4 CMLR 718

60 [2007] OJ L 32/23.

61 See R Whish and D Bailey, *Competition Law* (Oxford University Press 2019) 801; J Killick, 'IMS and Microsoft Judged in the Cold Light of IMS' (2004) 1(2) Competition Law Review 23–47.

and leaves questions unanswered as to the impact of enforcement on innovation and dynamic efficiency.[62] The approach taken in Microsoft and the leap that was made in relation to the 'new product' criterion developed in earlier case law risks discouraging innovation by eroding the value of intellectual property. Until a case presenting similar issues is brought by the CMA, it is hard to predict the approach to be adopted in the UK. However, it is worth noting that interference with property rights has occurred in UK competition law through the use of market investigations – most notably the 2009 decision to order the British Airport Authority to sell a number of its airports to create competition.[63]

Dynamic efficiency and the treatment of Big Tech – The regulation of big technology firms is an issue that is currently preoccupying a number of governments in relation to competition but also other policy areas such as data protection and incitement to violence. There is a growing recognition that traditional competition law tools may not be enough to challenge the dominance of firms like Google or Facebook. However, there is significant disagreement as to how the problem should be approached. For example, while some argue for direct regulation, others suggest the focus should be on creating the economic conditions that make it more likely new firms can challenge the tech incumbents.[64] The issue has sparked significant soul-searching among competition authorities, many of whom have produced detailed reports on competition in digital markets.[65] In the EU it has also culminated in the Digital Markets Act, which will not be adopted into UK law. In the UK, the CMA has shown a keen interest in the issue of competition in digital markets. In March 2019 HM Treasury published an independent report

---

62 See D Geradin, 'Limiting the Scope of Article 82 EC: What Can the EU Learn from the US Supreme Court's Judgement in *Trinko* in the Wake of *Microsoft, IMS and Deutsche Telekom*?' (2004) 41 Common Market Law Review 1519–1553.

63 Competition Commission, *BAA Airports Market Investigation: A Report on the Supply of Airport Services by BAA in the UK* (19 March 2009). The Competiton Commission was the UK's second competition authority before it and the OFT were merged into the CMA in 2014.

64 See in particular L Khan, 'The Separation of Platforms and Commerce' (2019) 119 Columbia Law Review 793; Tim Wu, *The Curse of Bigness: How Corporate Giants Came to Rule the World* (Atlantic Books 2020); and N Petit, *Big Tech and the Digital Economy: The Moligopoly Scenario* (Oxford University Press 2020).

65 See in particular European Commission, *Competition Policy for the Digital Era* (2019); United States Congress, *Investigation of Competition in Digital Markets*, Majority Staff Report and Recommendations, Subcommittee on Antitrust, Commercial and Administrative Law of the Committee on the Judiciary (2020).

on digital competition – 'The Furman Report'.[66] In implementing one of the report's key recommendations, in November 2020 the UK government announced the creation of a new Digital Markets Unit (DMU) within the CMA.[67] The DMU, established in April 2021, will oversee competition with platforms like Google and Facebook, and enforce a new code to govern their behaviour. In January 2021, the CMA opened an investigation into Google's 'privacy sandbox' browser settings under Chapter II of the Competition Act 1998. Accordingly, this is one area where the CMA and the UK are already forging their own regulatory approach and enforcement priorities.

While s.60A of the Competition Act widens the scope for a potentially divergent UK approach in relation to both agreements and abuse of dominance, this part of the chapter has demonstrated how that scope is considerably greater in relation to the latter. If the number of CMA Chapter II investigations does not increase, then UK law will remain aligned to pre-Brexit EU jurisprudence only by virtue of the UK standing still in this area. The aforementioned areas show considerable room for rival interpretation of abuse of dominance rules within the UK and EU regimes. Consequently, if the CMA investigates more Chapter II infringements, there is potential for UK competition law to develop in a different direction to that of the EU. Indeed, divergence of approach is now inevitable in relation to digital markets, as both regimes are pressing on with separate post-Brexit policies. Sources of soft law – such as CMA guidance and the extent to which it is different to that of the European Commission – could be a crucial early indicator of where any divergence may occur.

2.4 Sanctions against individuals involved in cartels

Cartels are considered to be the most damaging forms of anti-competitive behaviour and consequently, in addition to falling firmly into the 'object' category of Article 101, they can also attract criminal prosecution in a number of European jurisdictions, including the UK.[68] The rationale for the

---

66 Digital Competition Expert Panel, 'Unlocking Digital Competition' (Independent report, HM Treasury 2019).

67 HM Government Press Release, 'New Competition Regime for Tech Giants to Give Consumers More Choice and Control Over Their Data, and Ensure Businesses Are Fairly Treated' (27 November 2020).

68 See P Whelan, *The Criminalization of European Cartel Enforcement* (Oxford University Press 2014); and contributions to C Beaton-Wells and A Ezrachi (eds), *Criminalising Cartels: Critical Studies of an International Regulatory Movement* (Hart Publishing 2011);

introduction of criminal sanctions targeted at individuals is that deliber-
ate anti-competitive conduct is typically entered into by a small number of
individuals who go to great lengths to hide their behaviour from customers
and even their employers. There has been considerable academic literature
which has questioned the extent to which corporate fines alone provide a
sufficient deterrent to cartel participation without also some personal consequences of breaking the law for those individuals directly involved.[69] As
discussed in the introductory chapter, the UK's decision to criminalise cartel conduct was influenced by the success of US antitrust enforcement in
this area, and a sense that the EU's corporate penalties–only approach to
enforcement did not achieve effective deterrence.

The UK's criminal cartel offence has had a troubled history. Under s.188
of the Enterprise Act, it became a criminal offence for two or more individuals to *dishonestly agree* to make or implement a cartel agreement. This mirrored the approach taken in the law of theft and fraud, where the dishonest
nature of the alleged conduct is usually obvious. The offence was underuti-
lised primarily because it only applied to individuals and existed alongside
a purely administrative enforcement regime that concerned businesses. This
made it difficult to bring criminal cases because they were more time-consuming, costlier and less certain than administrative ones.[70] They had the
effect of holding up those administrative proceedings involving the businesses until any criminal trial was complete. It was also perceived that there
would be significant problems in demonstrating *dishonesty* to the satisfac-
tion of a jury – especially where the cartel might have been primarily motivated by crisis rather than greed.[71] The Enterprise and Regulatory Reform
Act 2013 removed the requirement to prove dishonesty and introduced a set
of carve-outs and defences broadly designed to exclude practices entered
into openly.[72] No criminal cases have been prosecuted under the reformed
offence to date. Indeed, in a letter written by the (then) CMA chairman,

---

and KJ Cseres, MP Schinkel and FOW Vogelaar (eds), *Criminalization of Competition Law
Enforcement* (Edward Elgar 2006).

69 For a full discussion of the UK's cartel offence, see M O'Kane, *The Law of Criminal
Cartels: Practice and Procedure* (Oxford University Press 2009); M Furse and S Nash,
The Cartel Offence (Hart Publishing 2004); C Harding and J Joshua, *Regulating Cartels in
Europe* (Oxford University Press 2010) Chapter XI.

70 A Stephan, 'How Dishonesty Killed the Cartel Offence' (2011) 6 *Criminal Law Review*
446–455.

71 This was demonstrated by the acquittal of two defendants in *R v Dean and Stringer* (2015),
Southwark Crown Court, unreported. In this case the defence provided no evidence and did
not contest the facts – the defendants only denied dishonesty.

72 A Stephan, 'The UK Cartel Offence: A Purposive Interpretation?' (2014) 12 *Criminal Law
Review* 879–892.

Lord Tyrie, in February 2019, it was suggested that the CMA might relinquish its responsibility for criminal cartel enforcement altogether.[73]

Membership of the EU certainly did little to facilitate criminal prosecutions. One odd consequence of Article 101 TFEU being a purely administrative prohibition is that criminal sanctions within Member States can only, in effect, be applied to local infringements and not to the most damaging international cartels dealt with by the European Commission. Furthermore, there is no mechanism through which a Member State can hold up a Commission investigation pending the conclusion of criminal proceedings under national law.[74] Indeed, information received by a national competition authority through the ECN cannot be used as evidence in a criminal prosecution that could result in a custodial sentence, although it can be used to guide that investigation.[75] The problem is compounded by the obligation to apply Article 101 alongside national competition law, where a domestic case may affect trade between Member States.[76]

Leaving the EU gives the UK greater freedom to redesign and apply the criminal offence as it considers appropriate. In particular, it will be free to open a criminal investigation into a cartel that is also subject to a parallel administrative investigation by the European Commission, although that could have an impact on the level of cooperation the CMA receives from the Commission, as discussed in Chapter 1. One possibility is to extend criminal liability to the firm as well as the individuals responsible. The US experience has shown that the desire among businesses to settle their liability as swiftly as possible spurs on cooperation and admissions of guilt by the individuals responsible, albeit through a system of plea bargaining that cannot be copied directly under the respective criminal law processes of

---

73 Letter from The Rt Hon Lord Tyrie, Chairman of the CMA, to The Rt Hon Greg Clark MP, Secretary of State for Business, Energy and Industrial Strategy (21 February 2019), p. 6.

74 The only exception to this, the case of *Marine Hoses*, involving the arrest by the US Department of Justice of three UK nationals, who subsequently agreed to plead guilty to the UK cartel offence under a negotiated plea agreement with the US authorities. The case was concluded before the Commission proceeded with its investigation. See Andreas Stephan, 'How Dishonesty Killed the Cartel Offence' (2011) 6 Criminal Law Review 446; and *Marine Hoses* (Case COMP/39.406) [2009] OJ C 168/6.

75 Regulation 1/2003, Article 12.

76 This is pursuant to Regulation 1/2003, Article 3(1). In such circumstances, the UK has long maintained that the cartel offence does not constitute 'national competition law' and is therefore not under an obligation to also apply Article 101; see Department of Trade and Industry, *A World Class Competition Regime* (White Paper, CM 5233, 2001), para 10.16; confirmed by the English Court of Appeal in *IB* v *The Queen* [2009] EWCA Crim 2575.

the separate legal systems in the UK.[77] One interesting model the UK may wish to follow is that of Australia. Unlike the US, where all serious cartel infringements are treated as criminal, Australia has a 'dual proceedings' model under which criminal and civil sanctions can be imposed against businesses and individuals. The authority can therefore choose whether to pursue a criminal or civil process in a given case, while ensuring both the businesses and individuals responsible face some level of punishment.[78] Indeed, in principle, the Australian Competition and Consumer Commission (ACCC) could have two bites at the cherry, by attempting a criminal case in the first instance and then falling back on a civil case if it fails, although this has been criticised as amounting to double jeopardy.[79]

Nonetheless, it appears that any increase in criminal prosecutions under the cartel offence is unlikely in the immediate future, as it would only heighten the CMA's challenge of dealing with a significantly increased workload. It is more likely instead that the CMA will continue to expand the use of civil sanctions against individuals.[80] S.204 of the Enterprise Act amended the Company Directors Disqualification Act 1986 (CDDA), creating the 'Competition Disqualification Order'. While the use of the criminal offence has waned, resort to director disqualification in competition cases has been expanded in recent years.[81] Another possible alternative to criminal enforcement is the use of administrative fines against individuals as well as businesses – something that is not currently possible under the Competition Act 1998. This would constitute further policy divergence between the UK and EU, and could create further complexities for cooperation, where the UK chooses to name and sanction individuals whose identity is redacted in decisions by the European Commission.

2.5 The challenge of green competition law

One of the most significant challenges to the existing competition law orthodoxy in relation to horizontal agreements could come from the emerging

77 A Stephan, 'The Bankruptcy Wildcard in Cartel Cases' (2006) 5 Journal of Business Law 511.
78 Caron Beaton-Wells and Brent Fisse, *Australian Cartel Regulation: Law, Policy and Practice in an International Context* (CUP 2011) para 9.3.3.
79 ibid.
80 A Stephan, 'Disqualification Orders for Directors Involved in Cartels' (2011) 2(6) Journal for European Competition Law & Practice 529–536.
81 P Whelan, 'The Emerging Contribution of Director Disqualification in UK Competition Law' in B Rodger, P Whelan and A MacCulloch (eds), *The UK Competition Regime: A Twenty-Year Retrospective* (Oxford University Press 2021).

debate on how competition law can help encourage more sustainable use of resources and reduce emissions associated with climate change.[82] A key issue concerns the relatively narrow traditional focus of the consumer welfare standard (i.e. price, quality and innovation), which has become the core tenet of competition law analysis. Competition authorities are becoming increasingly worried that they will find themselves on the wrong side of history if competition analysis does not also start taking into account longer-term environmental or societal effects.[83] Certainly, we can characterise business behaviour that ignores sustainability goals as a form of market failure that is compounded by competition policy, because the negative externalities of competitive behaviour are not reflected in the price paid by consumers.[84] Those advocating an effects-based approach would argue that competition law is the wrong tool for capturing these externalities and that it is for government to address these concerns through taxation and subsidies. The issue is that any kind of balancing of anti-competitive effects against longer-term sustainability objectives that are hard to measure or reliably predict will cause problems – in particular by eroding the economic effects-based ethos of modern UK and EU competition law. In the context of Article 101, it may also require either a revised approach to applying the 'object' category of behaviour that is assumed to be anti-competitive, or the more liberal application of Article 101(3).[85]

There is also the issue of competitors entering into formal joint ventures to pursue research and development of green technologies, agreeing to minimum standards of sustainability in supply chains, or coordinating resources to reduce waste.[86] Many of these sorts of agreements already benefit from the block exemption regulation on research and development, but it could be argued that the gateways here do not go far enough in allowing competitors to exchange the levels of information that might be necessary

82 See J Nowag, *Environmental Integration in Competition and Free-Movement Laws* (OUP 2016); and S Holmes, 'Climate Change and Competition Law' OECD Hearing on Sustainability and Competition, 1 December 2020.

83 A Reston and M Sansom, 'Green Competition Law – Sustainable Collaboration or Anticompetitive Collusion?' (6 August 2020), Freshfields Bruckhaus Deringer LLP.

84 CA Volpin, 'Sustainability as a Quality Dimension of Competition: Protecting Our Future (Selves)' (2020) 1(2) Antitrust Chronicle Special Edition on Sustainability 9–18.

85 See discussion in S Holmes, 'Climate Change Is an Existential Threat: Competition Law Must Be Part of the Solution and Not Part of the Problem' (2020) 1(2) Antitrust Chronicle Special Edition on Sustainability 25–40.

86 See the special COVID-19 Edition of Journal of Antitrust Enforcement (June 2020) and in particular P Ormosi and A Stephan, 'The Dangers of Allowing Greater Coordination between Competitors during the COVID-19 Crisis' (2020) 8(2) Journal of Antitrust Enforcement 299–301.

to pursue environmental goals. The challenge for policymakers is realising this goal in a proportionate way and ensuring strict limits on the exchange of commercially sensitive information that could lead to anti-competitive outcomes. This is especially challenging given that collaboration on issues like sustainability may necessitate some exchange of information on aspects of production, efficiency or cost. The sharing of this knowledge cannot be reversed or controlled once the joint venture comes to an end. For example, in a highly concentrated market, it could make tacit coordination or oligopoly-type outcomes more likely. Worse still, it could help facilitate a hard-core cartel. Indeed it is not uncommon for cartel infringements to have developed from initial legitimate exchanges on issues such as safety and environmental standards, often at the encouragement of a government department or regulator.[87]

Competition authorities have already started moving towards providing greater assurances and guidance as to the types of sustainability agreements that will not be actioned under national or EU law. The Dutch Authority for Consumers and Markets (ACM) announced in July 2020 the publication of a draft consultation document on sustainability.[88] This included 'agreements that incentivize undertakings to make a positive contribution to a sustainability objective without being binding on individual undertakings' and 'agreements that are aimed at improving product quality, while, at the same time, certain products that are produced in a less sustainable manner are no longer sold'.[89] In January 2021, the ACM published its revised draft sustainability guidelines, which gave greater weight to pro-sustainability benefits when considering the legality of an agreement.[90] Such moves could develop into a significant area of evolution for antitrust rules, with the emergence of further cut-outs or 'comfort guidance' in relation to certain types of coordination. This may of course conflict with the Dutch competition authority's obligations to enforce national competition law in a way that is consistent

87 See, for example, comments made by Tesco in relation to the OFT's dairy price fixing case: 'Tesco Prepares to Fight Charges of Collusion in Price Fixing Scandal' *The Times* (8 December 2007) and also CMA, *Galvanised Steel Tanks for Water Storage* (18 December 2016) CE/9691/12 at 3.5.

88 Autoriteit Consument & Markt, *Guidelines: Sustainability Agreements: Opportunities within Competition Law* (9 July 2020) www.acm.nl/sites/default/files/documents/2020-07/sustainability-agreements%5B1%5D.pdf (accessed 19 August 2020).

89 ibid, 7.

90 Autoriteit Consument & Markt, Guidelines: Sustainability Agreements: Opportunities within Competition Law (Second Draft, January 2021). https://www.acm.nl/sites/default/files/documents/second-draft-version-guidelines-on-sustainability-agreements-oppurtunities-within-competition-law.pdf (accessed 26 May 2021).

with EU law. However, the European Commission appeared to be support-ive of this Dutch approach, indicating its full support and suggested similar guidance may be on the horizon at the EU level.[91] Some commentators are already flagging these moves as signalling a weakening of the core prohi-bitions under EU competition law.[92] Spurred on by the disruption caused by the Covid pandemic, regulators may soon begin questioning the very assumption that competition usually results in the best outcomes for mar-kets and consumers.[93] Sustainability has also been identified as a priority by the CMA,[94] which in January 2021 published a guidance document to help prevent competition law from having a chilling effect on legitimate sustain-ability agreements.[95] When interviewed about the Dutch ACM guidelines, the chairman of the ACM, Martijn Snoep, said, 'admittedly, the EU courts have never explicitly endorsed this approach but at the same time, they have never ruled to the contrary either'.[96]

2.6 Concluding remarks on antitrust

The UK's core antitrust enforcement rules can be seamlessly applied to all anti-competitive conduct affecting UK markets. The most immediate and obvious challenges relate to the resourcing and workload of the CMA and the need to quickly develop the expertise and bilateral relationships needed to be an effective global competition authority. The close links between UK and EU competition law ensure a good level of legal certainty for businesses, especially as block exemptions have been adopted into UK law and given the obligation to follow pre-Brexit EU case law. However, the new s.60A of the Competition Act allows UK authorities and courts to depart from exist-ing EU competition law where there is a good justification. This is not con-strained by the provisions of the Trade and Cooperation Agreement, which

---

91 European Commission, 'Statement on ACM Public Consultation on Sustainability Guidelines' (9 July 2020). 'Antitrust: What's New?' https://ec.europa.eu/competition/an titrust/news.html (accessed 19 August 2020).

92 MP Schinkel and A d'Ailly, 'Corona Crisis Cartels: Sense and Sensibility' (12 June 2020) Amsterdam Centre for Law & Economics Working Paper No. 2020-03.

93 For a discussion of this, see M Stucke, 'Is Competition Always Good?' (2013) 1(1) Journal of Antitrust Enforcement 162–197.

94 Reston and Sansom, p. 2, citing the CMA's 2020/21 Annual Report, which noted that it is 'essential that in delivering our statutory functions, we act in a way which supports the transition to a low carbon economy'.

95 CMA Guidance, *Environmental Sustainability Agreements and Competition Law* (27 January 2021).

96 'Interview with Martijn Snoep' (2020) 1(2) Antitrust Chronicle Special Edition on Sustainability 7–8.

merely set out an obligation to continue applying antitrust in general terms only. The flexibility created by s.60A will not be welcomed by those who advocated a stronger continued link between UK and EU competition rules. However, the CMA and the CAT are very unlikely to exercise the freedoms provided by s.60A in relation to clear and settled questions of competition law, which by their nature do not tend to change according to jurisdiction. They will maintain a watching brief on the post-Brexit development of EU case law and are very likely to be strongly influenced by it. Nonetheless, divergence in the interpretation and application of aspects of the substantive rules of UK and EU competition law is probably inevitable by virtue of the fact so many aspects of the scope and application of the law are still evolving or are unresolved, and whose effects (and therefore correct treatment in law) are still disputed by academics, as discussed in this chapter. Abuse of dominance, the regulation of digital markets and the possibility of expanded exclusions for anti-competitive agreements that pursue an environmental goal are key areas to watch in the coming years. Finally, divergence may also be driven simply by the CMA's new freedom to prioritise competition issues and markets that it considers to be of particular importance to UK consumers.

3 Private enforcement

3.1 Introduction

While the public enforcement of UK competition rules will expand as a consequence of Brexit, the level of private enforcement in the UK may actually shrink because so many actions for damages in the UK courts to date have been follow-on cases relating to European Union (EU) cartel decisions. As was discussed in the Introduction to this book, London had de facto become the forum of choice for such actions. In order to understand and analyse the potential impact of UK withdrawal from the EU on the private enforcement of competition law, we have to reflect on the legislation, institutions and case law developments which have created the current framework for parties to seek to enforce their competition law–based rights through normal litigation processes.

The chapter will briefly consider the crucial legal and institutional developments in private enforcement in the UK which have facilitated and encouraged competition law litigation in the exercise of the rights and obligations created by the competition law rules.[1] This will be followed by discussion of various particularly significant issues in the UK context which can enhance the availability of damages actions: the procedural rules on limitation; the binding effect of the national competition authority (NCA) and Commission decisions; effective disclosure mechanisms; the existence of a specialist court/tribunal; the availability of compensatory damages awards; the specific mechanisms instituted in relation to collective redress; and finally, the funding of private enforcement actions. A detailed discussion of these aspects will allow us to consider the extent to which the UK's withdrawal from the EU may have negative repercussions on the role

---

1 See B Rodger, 'UK Competition Law and Private Litigation' in B Rodger (ed), *Ten Years of UK Competition Law Reform* (Dundee University Press 2010) Chapter 3.

DOI: 10.4324/9781351105446-3

of the UK courts in providing an adequate system for effective competition law consumer redress in the UK.[2] Furthermore, in the final section we will consider three further significant issues with post-Brexit implications for private enforcement in the UK: the nature of EU law as a foreign law; the changes in private international rules, particularly in relation to civil and commercial jurisdiction; and the ongoing applicability of the Antitrust Damages Directive provisions.

3.2 Key legislative and institutional developments

3.2.1 UK statutory developments

It is worth beginning with a brief recap of the key statutory developments relating to private enforcement in the UK. There was very limited scope for any form of private enforcement of the UK's competition legislative provisions, until the Competition Act 1998 introduced the two key Chapter I and II prohibitions. They established conduct as illegal and consequently rights for parties to seek damages and injunctive relief if harmed by that infringing conduct. Subsequently, the Enterprise Act 2002 sought to facilitate private actions in the UK by introducing s.47A of the Competition Act 1998,[3] which provided for the Competition Appeal Tribunal (CAT)[4] to grant damages and other monetary awards where there was a finding of an infringement of the Chapters I or II prohibitions or Articles 101 or 102 TFEU.[5] It also added s.47B to the 1998 Act, allowing damages claims to be brought before the CAT by a specified body on behalf of two or more consumers with claims in respect of the same infringement[6] – a form of 'consumer representative action'.

Actions can be brought before either the CAT or the High Court, but the CAT was unable to hear stand-alone actions and non-monetary claims

---

2 See for example, A Howard, 'Brexit: Exit Stage Left for Competition Damages' (2018) Competition Law Journal Brexit Special Online Edition 4–9.

3 As introduced by s.18 of the Enterprise Act.

4 For a fuller discussion of the CAT, see D Bailey 'The Early Case-Law of the Competition Appeal Tribunal' in B. Rodger (ed), *Ten Years of UK Competition Law Reform* (Dundee University Press 2010) Chapter 2.

5 See M Furse 'Follow-On Actions in the UK; Litigating Section 47A of the Competition Act 1998' (2013) 9(1) European Competition Journal 79–103. Note s.47A has been revised to refer only to infringements of the Chapter I and II prohibitions by the Competition (Amendment etc.) (EU Exit) Regulations 2019, SI 2019/93.

6 Ss.47B(1) and (4).

prior to the Consumer Rights Act 2015 reforms.[7] Given that claims against multiple parties often combine stand-alone and follow-on elements, such claims were outside the CAT's jurisdiction and had to be raised before the High Court.[8] Another rationale for a claim being raised before the High Court related to the fact that a CAT action could not be raised until all public enforcement appeal processes had been finalised.[9] The Consumer Rights Act 2015 made various amendments to the Competition Act regime as of 1 October 2015 to enhance the role of the CAT as the specialist forum for competition law disputes in the UK. The act also introduced an opt-out collective redress mechanism in relation to competition law infringements.[10] It is important to note in a chapter dedicated to consideration of the impact of UK withdrawal from the EU, that it is difficult to separate private competition law enforcement in the UK from the wider European context, in which there have been considerable EU developments which have impacted on the availability and success of remedies in competition litigation.

3.2.1 EU law developments

There have been a number of important developments over the last 25 years or more to encourage private enforcement of competition law, such as the Commission Notice on Co-operation with the National Courts in 1993,[11] the European Court of Justice's (CJEU) *Crehan* and *Manfredi* rulings,[12] the introduction of Regulation 1/2003,[13] and the adoption of the Antitrust

---

7　S.47A(10) of the 1998 Act. See for example *Devenish Nutrition Ltd v Sanofi-Aventis SA (France)*, [2007] EWHC 2394 (Ch) and [2008] EWCA Civ 1086 (CA). The CRA 2015 came into force as of 1 October 2015, the Consumer Rights Act 2015 (Commencement No. 3, Transitional Provisions, Savings and Consequential Amendments) Order 2015 SI 2015/1630.

8　See for instance *Cooper Tire & Rubber Co v Shell Chemicals UK Ltd* [2010] EWCA Civ 864, CA. See also *Nokia Corporation v AU Optonics Corporation and others* [2012] EWHC 732 (Ch) and *Toshiba Carrier UK Ltd and others v KME Yorkshire Ltd and others* [2011] EWHC 2665 (Ch).

9　*Emerson III* [2008] CAT 8 involving claims against parties who had appealed to the General Court.

10　See A Andreangeli, 'The Changing Structure of Competition Enforcement in the UK: The Competition Appeal Tribunal between Present Challenges and an Uncertain Future' (2015) Journal of Antitrust Enforcement 1–30. See B Rodger, 'The Consumer Rights Act 2015 and Collective Redress for Competition Law Infringements in the UK: A Class Act?' (2015) 3(2) Journal of Antitrust Enforcement 258–286.

11　[1993] OJ C39/6.

12　Case C-453/99 *Courage v Crehan* [2001] ECR I-6297; Case C-295/04 *Manfredi v Lloyd Adriatico Assicurazioni SpA* [2006] ECR I-6619.

13　[1993] OJ L 1/4.

Damages Directive in 2014.[14] The Commission's focus in this area has been on damages actions.[15] The CJEU has also played a fundamental role in shaping the development of competition litigation across the EU in a range of preliminary rulings on rights and remedies generally under EU law,[16] and specifically in relation to EU competition law.[17] EU law requires Member States to provide effective protection of rights granted under EU law to individuals against their violation by other individuals.[18] The European Court's role and influence in relation to remedies for infringement of EU law was exemplified by its rulings in the *Crehan* and *Manfredi* cases in the English and Italian courts. As emphasised, the principle of the effectiveness of EU law rights is fundamental for national courts in dealing with claims (or defences) based on EU competition law and it also underpins the Antitrust Damages Directive[19] in the context of damages actions – particularly in Articles 3 and 4 (the principles of effectiveness and equivalence). The effectiveness principle was re-emphasised in *Kone AG v OBB-Infrastruktur AG*,[20] although the shift to recognition of the constituent elements of a damages claim as arising directly from EU law in the recent case law[21] is clear and is likely to continue.

In the UK, the Antitrust Damages Directive was implemented by the Damages Directive Statutory Instrument – Claims in respect of Loss or Damage arising from Competition Infringements (Competition Act 1998 and other Enactments (Amendment) Regulations 2017 ('the

14 Commission Recommendation of 11 June 2013 on common principles for injunctive and compensatory collective mechanisms [2013] OJ L 201/60.
15 See V Milutonivic, *Right to Damages' Under EU Competition Law* (Kluwer Law International 2010). See B Rodger (ed), *Competition Law Comparative Private Enforcement and Collective Redress across the EU* (Kluwer Law International 2014).
16 See B Rodger, *Article 234 and Competition Law: An Analysis* (Kluwer Law International 2008).
17 See for instance *Wyatt and Dashwood's European Union Law* (Hart Publishing 2014), particularly Chapters 7–9.
18 See Case 127/73 *BRT v SABAM* [1974] ECR 51; Case 319/82, *Société de Vente de Ciments et Bétons de l'Est SA* v *Kerpen & Kerpen GmbH* [1983] 4173, para 12. See O Odudu and A Sanchez-Graells, 'The Interface of EU and National Tort Law: Competition Law' in P Giliker (ed), *Research Handbook on EU Tort Law* (Edward Elgar 2017) Chapter 6.
19 See N Dunne, 'The Role of Private Enforcement within EU Competition Law' (2014) 16 Cambridge Yearbook of European Legal Studies 143–187 at 157 and 181–182 in particular.
20 Case C-557/12 [2014] 5 CMLR. See for example G De Burca, 'National Procedure Rules and Remedies: The Changing Approach of the Court of Justice' in J Lonbay and A Biondi (eds), *Remedies for Breach of EC Law* (1997) 37; W Van Gerven, 'Of Rights, Remedies and Procedures' (2000) 37 Common Market Law Review 501–536.
21 See for example Case C-274/17 *Vantaan Kaupunka v Skanska Industrial Solutions Oy* (14 March 2019).

Regulations').[22] The Regulations apply to any competition damages claim where there is an infringement of any of the UK and/or EU prohibitions without any requirement for parallel application of EU and national law in the proceedings. Article 22(1) of the Directive states that the Member State shall ensure the national measures adopted to comply with the substantive provisions of the Directive 'do not apply retroactively' and Article 22(2) provides that they 'shall not apply to actions for damages for which a national court was seized prior to 26 December 2014'. Effectively, for the substantive provisions of the Directive, there will be a considerable lag before the implementing measures are effective and have any impact on competition damages actions before the UK courts. It should finally be noted that the implementing Regulations are to be treated as retained EU law (EU-derived domestic legislation under section 2 of the European Union (Withdrawal) Act 2018) and in force until such time as their Directive-derived provisions and effect are reviewed and revised.

3.3 Specific issues

This section of the chapter will address various core aspects of the private litigation architecture in the UK, which will help us to understand the likely impact of Brexit.

3.3.1 Limitation periods

The most significant procedural issue in practice concerns the application of the limitation rules in the competition law context.[23] English law generally allows for a six-year limitation period.[24] There is special provision for postponement of the limitation period in case of fraud, concealment or mistake under s.32 of the Limitation Act 1980. In such cases, the time limit will not run until the claimant has discovered the concealment or could have done so with reasonable diligence.[25] Those Limitation Act provisions

---

22 See HL Hansard (2 March 2017) Vol 779; B Rodger, 'United Kingdom' in B Rodger, M Sousa Ferro and P Marcos (eds), *The EU Antitrust Damages Directive, Transposition in the Member States* (Oxford University Press 2018).

23 See B Rodger, 'Implementation of the Antitrust Damages Directive in the UK: Limited Reform of the Limitation Rules?' (2017) 38(5) European Competition Law Review 219–227.

24 *Limitation Act* 1980 s.2. See also s.47A of the Competition Act 1998.

25 See *Arcadia Group Brands and others v Visa Inc and others* [2015] EWCA Civ 883. In Scotland, see Prescription and Limitation (Scotland) Act 1973 s.6 (and s.11(3)); and D Johnson, *Prescription and Limitation*, 2nd edn (W. Green/SULI 2012).

were considered by the English courts in a competition law context in *Arcadia v Visa*.[26] It was held that the level of information published by the Commission in 2001 and 2002 in separate parts of the public enforcement process was sufficient for the claimants to establish the key facts to satisfy the statement of claim test.[27] Article 10 of the Directive provides for a specialised set of limitation (and prescription) rules, bringing significant change to the determination of the periods for competition damages actions in relation to infringements of both EU and UK competition law. The introduction of a five-year limitation period is relatively insignificant in itself. The most significant reform relates to when the limitation period begins to run – the so-called 'trigger point'. First, this will not take place until after the illegal activity has ceased. The second significant deviation from existing practice concerns the claimant knowledge requirements that trigger the limitation period. Para 19(1) of the implementing Regulations states that the period begins on the later of the day the infringement ceases or the claimant acquires knowledge of the infringement. The latter occurs when the claimant first knows or could reasonably be expected to know:

(a) of the infringer's behaviour;
(b) that the behaviour constitutes an infringement of competition law;
(c) that the claimant has suffered loss or damage arising from that infringement; and
(d) the identity of the infringer.

The post-Directive rules certainly appear to recalibrate the procedural advantage in favour of claimants. It remains to be seen whether the constructive knowledge requirements will be retained. Nonetheless, the Court of Appeal very recently stressed, in *DSG v Mastercard*,[28] that the personal characteristics of the claimant may be relevant and the mere availability of documents in the public domain on the internet does not necessarily place a particular claimant on notice of a claim or mean they should with reasonable diligence have seen particular documents.[29]

---

26 *Arcadia Group Brands and others v Visa Inc and others* [2015] EWCA Civ 883.
27 See also *WH Newson Holding Ltd v IMI plc* High, [2015] EWHC 1676 (Ch) and [2016] EWCA Civ 773.
28 [2020] EWCA Civ 671 paras 63–71.
29 ibid at para 70.

3.3.2 Binding force of competition authority decisions

To ensure the follow-on damages mechanism before the CAT would have the greatest success in facilitating litigation,[30] provision was made regarding the binding nature of prior enforcement authority decisions.[31] Section 58A to the Competition Act 1998 provided that in any action for damages for an infringement of the Competition Act 1998 prohibitions or Articles 101(1) or 102 TFEU, a court will be bound by a decision of the CMA or CAT that any of the prohibitions have been infringed[32] if the requisite appeal process has taken place or the period for appeal lapsed.[33] The Consumer Rights Act revised the scope of s.58A of the Competition Act 1998, with effect from 1 October 2015 (in relation to decisions made after that date). It now provides that prior infringement decisions are binding both in relation to proceedings before the courts and the CAT under either s.47A or s.47B.[34] In addition, s.58A made final infringement decisions by the European Commission binding on the CAT and courts, but this rule has now been removed.[35] The Directive also contains a provision allowing Member State courts to refer to final infringement decisions taken in other Member States as *prima facie* evidence that a competition law infringement has occurred.[36] These beneficial aspects of the implementation of the Directive have been lost as a consequence of Brexit.

3.3.3 The existence of a specialist court/tribunal

The existence and functions allocated to a specialist competition court or tribunal are clearly major factors in the institutional design of a legal

30 See J Dodds and B Rayment, '*WH Newson Holding ltd and others v IMI Plc*: New Developments in the Jurisdiction of the UK Competition Appeal Tribunal' (2013) 34(8) European Competition Law Review 395–399, and also the subsequent Court of Appeal ruling [2013] EWCA Civ. 1377.

31 See for example M Sousa Ferro 'Antitrust Private Enforcement and the Binding Effect of Public Enforcement Decisions' (2019) 3(2) Market and Competition Law Review 51. See Court of Appeal in *Enron Coal Services Ltd (in Liquidation) v English, Welsh and Scottish Railway Ltd* [2011] EWCA Civ 2.

32 S.58A(2) of the Competition Act 1998.

33 S.58A(3). See also Article 16 of Regulation 1/2003 in relation to Commission decisions. See discussion in *Enron Coal Services Ltd (in Liquidation) v English, Welsh and Scottish Railway Ltd* [2011] EWCA Civ 2.

34 In relation to the CAT, the revised s.58A effectively replaced s.47A(9) of the 1998 Act.

35 S.58A(4). See Regulations 2019, SI 2019/93.

36 Article 9(2). See para 35 of the Implementing Regulations.

system to deal with competition litigation.[37] The Consumer Rights Act 2015 enhanced the role of the CAT as the specialist forum for competition law disputes in the UK.[38] A central aspect of the reform was the extension of the competence of the CAT under s.47A of the Competition Act 1998 to stand-alone actions in addition to 'follow-on' actions.[39] Furthermore, the CAT now has power (at least in proceedings in England and Wales and Northern Ireland) to grant injunctions.[40] The practical role of the CAT was significantly enhanced by the (belated) adoption of s.16 Enterprise Act Regulations 2015.[41] The 2015 Regulations allow the High Court to transfer cases to the CAT for its determination of 'so much of any proceedings as relates to an infringement issue'.[42] Nonetheless, despite the increasing significance of the CAT, the role of the appellate courts remains important. Indeed, the Supreme Court's developing involvement in competition litigation generally is notable, and it is likely to have an increasingly significant role in helping to shape the private enforcement landscape in the UK in the coming ten years. The increase in specialism in the courts of the UK may act as a bulwark to the threat that competition litigants will seek to raise their competition claims elsewhere following Brexit.

3.3.4 The availability of effective disclosure mechanisms

In England and Wales, the Civil Procedure Rules mandate that a party must disclose all documents which are relevant to the litigation, including those that harm its own case or support the opposing party's case.[43] There are

---

37 See D Bailey, 'The Early Case-Law of the Competition Appeal Tribunal', in B Rodger (ed), *Ten Years of UK Competition Law Reform* (Dundee University Press 2010) Chapter 2. See P Roth 'Specialized Antitrust Courts', in B Hawk (ed), *Annual Proceedings of the Fordham Competition Law Institute* (Fordham Competition Law Institute 2013) Chapter 7, 105.

38 See B Rodger, 'The Consumer Rights Act 2015 and Collective Redress for Competition Law Infringements in the UK: A Class Act?' (2015) 3(2) Journal of Antitrust Enforcement 258–286.

39 See P Akman 'Period of Limitations in Follow-On Competition Cases: When Does a Decision Become Final?' (2014) 2(2) Journal of Antitrust Enforcement 389–421. See Rule 119 of the revised CAT rules (The Competition Appeal Tribunal Rules 2015, SI 2015/1648). See *Gibson v Pride Mobility Products Ltd* [2017] CAT 9.

40 S.47A(3).

41 2015/1643.

42 S.16(6) of the Enterprise Act 2002.

43 Civil Procedure Rules Part 31; in particular Part 31.6(b). See Rules 60–65 of the Competition Appeal Tribunal Rules 2015.

limits on pre-trial disclosure,[44] but the disclosure mechanisms (particularly in England and Wales)[45] have been a significant factor in the historical attractiveness of the UK courts to litigation relating to multi-state competition law infringements. Article 5 of the Antitrust Damages Directive was aimed primarily at those Member States with limited provision for pre-trial disclosure.[46] The most controversial provision in the Directive concerned the protection of leniency applicants' documentation from access by claimants through court disclosure processes.[47] The limitations on access to leniency documentation had been examined by the European Court in *Pfleiderer*[48] and that ruling was considered and applied in *National Grid Electricity Transmission plc v ABB Ltd and others*.[49] The High Court confirmed that there could not be a 'blanket objection to disclosure',[50] and the courts would assess, on a document-by-document basis, the extent to which the materials sought are necessary for proving the damages claim.[51] Nonetheless, the Directive as implemented deviates from the CJEU jurisprudence and restricts access in private litigation to leniency documentation in a way which is unfortunately likely to limit claimant incentives and likelihood of success in follow-on claims.[52] There may potentially be consideration post-Brexit to excluding that rule and returning to the *Pfleiderer* approach as applied in *National Grid*.

---

44 See *Hutchison 3G UK ltd v O2 (UK) Ltd* [2008] EWHC 50 (Comm). See also Rule 18 of the CPR.

45 *National Grid Electricity Transmission Plc v ABB Ltd* [2014] EWHC 1055 (Ch). See also *Infederation Ltd v Google Inc* [2015] EWHC 3705 (Ch); *Peugeot and others v NSK Ltd* [2018] CAT 3, para 30, see also para 31. In Scotland note the process of specification of documents. If not forthcoming, Chapter 35 of the Court of Session Rules allow for an application for commission and diligence for recovery of documents to compel a party to disclose withheld documents.

46 CPR 31C and CAT practice direction relating to Disclosure and Inspection of Evidence in Claims made pursuant to Parts 4 and 5 of the Competition Appeal Tribunal Rules 2015.

47 See for example A Singh '*Pfleiderer*: Assessing Its Impact on the Effectiveness of the European Leniency Programme' (2014) 35(3) European Competition Law Review 110–123.

48 Case C-360/09 *Pfleiderer v AG Bundeskartellamt* [2011] ECR I-5161 paras 30 and 31. See also Case C-536/11, *Donau Chemie et. al.* [2013] 5 CMLR 19.

49 [2012] EWHC 869 (Ch).

50 ibid at para 50.

51 See NH Endendorf and N Maierhofer 'The Road after *Pfleiderer*' (2013) 34 European Competition Law Review 78.

52 See Article 6(6). See C Rey, 'The Interaction between Public and Private Enforcement of Competition Law, and Especially the Interaction between the Interests of Private Claimants and those of Leniency Applicants' (2015) 8(3) Global Competition Litigation Review 109–125. See Articles 6 and 7 of the Directive generally.

3.3.5 *Damages awards*

The underlying basis for the award of competition law damages, as with other types of tort or delict claim, is compensation for loss suffered.[53] Where claims based on EU competition law are concerned, this has been confirmed by the European Court jurisprudence in *Crehan* and *Manfredi*, and reaffirmed by Article 3 of the Antitrust Damages Directive, which highlights the right to full compensation based on the principles of equivalence and effectiveness.[54] The Antitrust Damages Directive contains various provisions regarding the extent of liability, passing-on, indirect purchasers and quantification of harm which seek to ensure the general effectiveness of the EU right to full compensation.

There has been some experience in the award and calculation of damages awards by both the CAT and High Court.[55] The general principles informing the calculation of the overcharge damages award[56] are compensation/reparation, the balance of probabilities and 'where there is an element of estimation and assumption – as frequently there will be – restoration by way of compensation is often accomplished by "sound imagination" and a "broad axe"'.[57] Nonetheless, the view that damages are awarded *only* for the purpose of compensation in the UK courts was rejected.[58] The Court of Appeal in *Devenish*[59] had indicated that the English courts should adopt a strictly compensatory approach and that there would be little scope for restitutionary, exemplary or other forms of multiple damages awards. Nevertheless, the CAT subsequently awarded £60k for exemplary damages in *2 Travel Group PLC*,[60] yet s.47C(1) of the Competition Act, introduced by the Consumer Rights Act, later proscribed the award of exemplary damages by the CAT in collective proceedings. Subsequently, the potential for exemplary damages in UK competition proceedings was

---

53 See S Peyer, 'Compensation and the Damages Directive' (2016) 12 European Competition Journal 87–112.

54 Article 4.

55 See *2 Travel Group PLC (in Liquidation) v Cardiff City Transport Services Ltd* [2012] CAT 19; *Albion Water v Dwr Cymru Cyfyngedig* [2013] CAT 6; *Sainsbury's Supermarkets Ltd v Mastercard Inc and others* [2016] CAT 11.

56 Para 423.

57 ibid. See also *Merricks v Mastercard* [2020] UKSC 51 at para 51.

58 J. Edelman, *Gain-Based Damages, Contract, Tort, Equity and Intellectual Property* (Hart Publishing 2002). See Lord Nicholls in *Att-Gen v Blake* [2001] 1 A.C. 268 at 285.

59 See *2 Travel Group PLC (in Liquidation) v Cardiff City Transport Services Ltd* [2012] CAT 19.

60 ibid. C Veljanovski 'CAT Awards Triple Damages, Well Not Really – *Cardiff Bus*, and the Dislocation between Liability and Damages for Exclusionary Abuse' (2012) 33 European Competition Law Review 47–49.

removed altogether by the implementing Regulations, which gave effect to the general prohibition of over-compensation contained in Article 3 of the Damages Directive.[61] It remains to be seen whether Brexit could open the door once more to the availability of exemplary damages – especially in relation to stand-alone claims where the absence of public enforcement means deterrence has not been served.

Chapter IV (Articles 12–14 in particular) of the Directive tackles the problematic issue of the passing-on of overcharges, specifically requiring changes in the UK to ensure the burden of proof was on the defendant in line with Article 13 of the Directive.[62] Moreover, an indirect purchaser would only need to establish: (i) an infringement by the defender; (ii) that it resulted in an overcharge to the direct purchaser; and (iii) the indirect purchaser has purchased goods or services which are the object of the infringement. There has been considerable academic literature in this context over the years,[63] though no case-law practice in the UK until *Sainsbury's Supermarkets Ltd v Mastercard Inc and others*,[64] in which there was considerable reflection by the CAT on the pass-on defence,[65] albeit the Directive was inapplicable. The CAT confirmed for the first time the recognition of overcharge claims by indirect purchasers and the existence of a passing-on defence for defendants.[66] The CAT stressed that:

> the pass-on 'defence' ought only to succeed where, on the balance of probabilities, the defendant has shown that there exists another class of claimant, downstream of the claimant(s) in the action, to whom the overcharge has been passed on. [Otherwise] we consider that a claimant's recovery of the overcharge incurred by it should not be reduced or defeated on this ground.[67]

---

61 See para 36 and Recital 13.
62 See B Rodger, 'United Kingdom' in B Rodger, M Sousa Ferro and P Marcos (eds), *The EU Antitrust Damages Directive, Transposition in the Member States* (Oxford University Press 2018).
63 See C Petrucci, 'The Issues of the Passing-on Defence and Indirect Purchasers' Standing in European Competition Law' (2008) 29 European Competition Law Review 33.
64 Case 1241/5/7/15 (T) *Sainsbury's Supermarkets Ltd v Mastercard Inc and others* [2016] CAT 11.
65 At paras 479 et seq. See in particular para 480.
66 Para 484.
67 ibid. The Supreme Court subsequently stressed that the evidentiary burden did not require a greater degree of precision on the part of the defendants (than the claimants) in quantifying the precise level of pass-on made by the claimants [2020] UKSC 24 at paras 175–226, particularly paras 225–226.

It is unlikely that Brexit will lead to any particular divergences in this approach.

3.3.6 Collective redress mechanism

It is generally recognised that effective justice requires appropriate collective redress mechanisms to ensure that consumers are compensated where the harm resulting from the anti-competitive conduct is widely dispersed or otherwise passed on to final consumers.[68] Yet the specialist representative follow-on action introduced by s.47B of the Competition Act 1998 had clear limitations, most notably the low participation rates in opt-in schemes due to a lack of incentives.[69] Subsequently, the Consumer Rights Act 2015 amended s.47B to provide for both opt-out and opt-in collective proceedings before the CAT, although the difficulties in obtaining successful collective redress for consumers has been demonstrated by the first two cases under the new regime – *Gibson* and *Merricks*. In *Gibson v Pride Mobility*, the CAT rejected the proposed definition of the applicant's class and the methodology used to formulate them.[70]

In *Merricks v Mastercard*,[71] the claims were held by the CAT not to be certifiable under Rule 79 of the Tribunal Rules as eligible for inclusion in collective proceedings. The claim was for an aggregate sum of circa £14 billion including interest and the class was considered to be around 46.2 million people. The case failed on the suitability test on the basis that the applicant had failed to put forward: (i) a sustainable methodology to be applied in practice to calculate a sum which reflected the aggregate of the individual claims; and (ii) a reasonable and practicable means for establishing the individual loss to be used a basis for distribution.[72] On appeal, the Court of Appeal rejected the CAT's reasoning and adopted a more

---

68 See for instance R Mulheron, *The Class Action in Common Law Legal Systems: A Comparative Perspective* (Hart Publishing 2004); R Mulheron, 'Recent Milestones in Class Actions Reform in England: A Critique and a Proposal' (2011) 127 Law Quarterly Review 288–315; R Mulheron, 'Opting In, Opting Out, and Closing the Class: Some Dilemmas for England's Class Actions Law-Makers' (2011) 50 Canadian Business Law Journal 376–408. See also M Ioannidou, *Consumer Involvement in Private EU Competition Law Enforcement* (Oxford University Press 2015).

69 See M Hviid and J Peysner, 'Comparing Economic Incentives across EU Member States' in B Rodger (ed), *Competition Law: Comparative Private Enforcement and Collective Redress across the EU* (Kluwer 2014).

70 [2017] CAT 9.

71 [2017] CAT 16.

72 S Peyer, 'Has the CAT's MasterCard Decision Killed Off Opt-Out Class Actions by Indirect Purchasers?' Competition Policy Blog (10 August 2017).

purposive approach to certification proceedings, recalibrating the process in favour of potential collective redress applicants. The ruling emphasised the need for the practical effectiveness of the collective proceedings scheme which should not create insurmountable barriers to collective redress by consumers.[73] The leading judgment by Lord Briggs in the Supreme Court confirmed the Court of Appeal's ruling that the CAT had erred in law on the first issue of quantification of aggregated losses and returned the application for a collective proceedings order (CPO) to the CAT.[74]

Despite early case-law setbacks in *Gibson* and *Merricks*, there are a number of ongoing CPO application proceedings before the CAT, notably in relation to numerous follow-on claims against Mastercard and Visa and in relation to the trucks cartel.[75] Hopefully the favourable ruling by the majority of the Supreme Court in *Merricks* on the level of precision and detail required for certification of CPO applications will incentivise future consumer-based claims to be instituted. In particular, the judgment clarifies that the complexity of quantification and any lack of data should not be a barrier to certification.[76]

3.3.7 Funding private enforcement

The availability of contingency fees for lawyers in the US has been central in incentivising the raising of class actions on behalf of consumers,[77] and its importance for any effective opt-out system has been stressed.[78] In England and Wales, there has been a considerable shift in the use of alternative legal fee arrangements over the last 15 years.[79] The Damages-Based Agreements Regulations 2013[80] allowed fees to be contingent upon the success of the claim and are calculated as a percentage of the compensation received by the claimant. These have been permissible generally in civil cases to incentivise lawyers to pursue riskier, work-intensive cases. In Scots law, the award of

---

73 [2019] EWCA Civ 674.

74 [2020] UKSC 51.

75 See generally www.catribunal.org.uk/cases (accessed 21 May 2021).

76 See S Peyer, 'Merricks Judgement Marks a Turning Point for UK Opt-Out Collective Actions' Competition Policy Blog (20 January 2021).

77 See for instance KC Wildfang and SP Slaughter 'Funding Litigation' in AA Foer and RM Stutz (eds), *Private Enforcement of Antitrust Law in the United States: A Handbook* (Edward Elgar 2012) Chapter 10.

78 C Hodges, J Peysner and A Nurse, 'Litigation Funding: Status and Issues' Joint Report University of Oxford & University of Lincoln (sponsored by Swiss Re) (2012).

79 ibid. Review of Civil Litigation Costs: Final Report, December 2009, www.judiciary.g ov.uk/wp-content/uploads/JCO/Documents/Reports/jackson-final-report-140110.pdf (accessed 21 May 2021).

80 SI 2013/609.

costs generally flows from success. Most litigation in Scotland is funded by the parties themselves. However, solicitors may enter into speculative fee agreements whereby the client is only liable to pay the solicitor's fees if the litigation is successful.[81] Scots law also allows third-party funding of litigation.[82] Following the Taylor Report,[83] the Civil Litigation (Expenses and Group Proceedings) (Scotland) Act 2018 makes provision for success fee agreements and third-party funding of litigation.[84]

Section 47C(8) of the amended Competition Act provides that 'a damages-based agreement is unenforceable if it relates to opt-out collective proceedings'.[85] Accordingly, a central conundrum is how prospective opt-out collective proceedings can be financed. The government accepted that third-party funding may be necessary to ensure effective consumer redress.[86] The only explicit arrangement for fees in opt-out collective actions can be found in s.47C(6) of the Competition Act 1998 (as amended by the Consumer Rights Act) and CAT r.93(4). These rules provide a route for costs and success fees to be recovered after the class members have received their damages, and the dicta in *Gibson* and *Merricks*[87] on the specific costs issues were positive from a third-party funding perspective. Again, irrespective of withdrawal, and in comparison with other Member State legal systems, there appear to be existing legal and practical benefits in funding arrangements for actions in the UK courts.

3.4 Direct impact of UK withdrawal from the EU

In the previous section, we examined key features of the UK private enforcement system and their likely continued post-Brexit significance. In that context the Competition (Amendment etc.) (EU Exit) Regulations

---

81 Allowed for by 61A of the Solicitors (Scotland) Act 1980.
82 *Quantum Claims Compensation Specialists Ltd v Powell* 1998 SC 316.
83 See Review of Expenses and Funding of Civil Litigation in Scotland, Report by Sh PJA Taylor, September 2013, available at http://scotland.gov.uk/About/Review/taylor-review/Report (accessed 21 May 2021).
84 In ss.1 and 10 respectively.
85 Amending s.58AA of the Courts and Legal Services Act 1990. See Rule 113 of the CAT rules 2015. See R Mulheron, 'The Damages-Based Agreements Regulations 2013: Some Conundrums in the "Brave New World" of Funding' (2013) 32 Civil Justice Quarterly 241–255.
86 Baroness Neville-Rolfe, Grand Committee, House of Lords, 3rd November 2014, col. 582. See *Merricks v Mastercard*, [2017] CAT 16 at para 127. A key concern, alleviated in that ruling, concerned the recovery of success fees and ATE premiums from the losing defendant.
87 *Merricks v Mastercard*, [2017] CAT 16 and *Gibson v Pride Mobility Products Ltd* [2017] CAT 9 at para 145.

2019[88] have made some consequential amendments, for instance limiting the scope of s.47A claims to Chapter I and Chapter II infringements and likewise restricting the scope of s.58A to CMA infringement decisions, where they relate to conduct occurring after Brexit. There are also three further key factors which may have direct implications for the continued role of the CAT (and High Court) as a key international forum for international competition litigation despite Brexit.[89]

The first category of issues concerns the scope and effect of EU competition law. First, EU law will no longer have direct effect and will be treated as a foreign law, with implications for the burden and cost of proof for party litigants, who will proceed by way of stand-alone claim based on breach of a foreign tort. This may, in theory, require EU law to be treated as a foreign law, which would need to be pled and proven in any claim proceedings.[90] This is normally undertaken by expert witnesses, leading to considerable expense and often a clash of experts. Probably more significant in practice, s.58A of the Competition Act has been revised to the effect that EU Commission decisions delivered after Brexit will no longer be binding on the CAT and courts in the UK.[91] These changes are likely to limit the incentives of litigating EU-wide (and beyond) cartels in the UK, also making it more difficult for consumers to raise collective actions based on prior Commission infringement decisions. However, given EU infringement decisions to 31 December 2020 can continue to be relied on, there will be a considerable time lag before this change has any real impact.

Second, the private international law rules within the EU have a considerable role to play in determining the rights and obligations arising out of anti-competitive activity, particularly in relation to wide-scale international cartels.[92] It is fundamental that a claimant can assert jurisdiction over a defendant before a particular court in order to raise an

---

88 SI 2019/93.

89 See also for instance Brexit Competition Law Working Group, *Conclusions and Recommendations* (July 2017) paras 2.17–2.27, also now published as J Fingleton et al., 'The Implications of Brexit for UK Competition Law and Policy' (2017) 13(3) Journal of Competition Law & Economics 389–422; See also A Robertson, 'The common law doctrine of restraint of trade – will it rise up again unshackled by Brexit and reformed by the Supreme Court? [2021] 42(2) ECLR 62–64.

90 See R Fentiman, *Foreign Law in English Courts* (Oxford University Press 1998).

91 Regulation 20, The Competition (Amendment etc) (EU Exit) Regulations 2019, SI 2019/93.

92 See B Rodger, 'EU Competition Law and Private International Law: A Developing Relationship' in I Lianos and D Geradin (eds), *Handbook on European Competition Law: Enforcement and Procedure* (Edward Elgar 2013) Chapter 8. See also J Basedow, S Francq and I Idot (eds), *International Antitrust Litigation, Conflict of Laws and Coordination* (Hart Publishing 2011).

action there in the first place. Moreover, claimants want to ensure that there are relatively straightforward and speedy rules to allow for the recognition and enforcement of a damages award judgment in the courts of other States where the defendant's funds and bank accounts may be based. The rules determining the civil jurisdiction of the courts in the EU, and consequently where in the EU an action based on a competition law infringement may be raised, are provided in the recast Brussels Ia Regulation.[93] This allowed any claimants, foreign or domestic, to raise an action in the courts of the UK on the basis that they could establish jurisdiction under the Brussels Ia Regulation and there have been numerous rulings by the CAT and High Court on aspects of the provisions of the regulation in a competition law context.[94] In this respect, the territorial scope of EU law infringements no longer extend to the UK,[95] and this may limit the jurisdiction of the courts here in certain cases. Given that the Brussels Ia Regulation is based on reciprocity, and in the absence of ongoing reciprocal arrangements, the post-Brexit Brussels regime has ceased to apply in the UK,[96] and accordingly the diverse and distinctive national rules of the different legal systems of the UK will apply to determine the jurisdiction of the courts and the CAT.[97] The Rome II Regulation[98] provides rules for determining the applicable law in non-contractual obligations and it will nonetheless continue to apply.[99] However, the significance of the Brussels Ia Regulation, and the relative attractiveness of the English courts as a forum for international competition litigation, rests in the rules of automatic recognition and enforcement of judgments under the regulation, where for instance a defendant is domiciled and has assets in another EU jurisdiction. The reciprocal nature of the EU-wide recognition and enforcement provisions under the Brussels

93 Regulation 1215/2012, [2012] OJ L 351/1.
94 See *Roche Products Limited v Provimi Limited* [2003] EWHC 961 (Comm); *Emerson Electric Co v Mersen UK Portslade Limited* [2012] EWCA Civ 1557 *Deutsche Bahn AG v Morgan Crucible co plc and others* Case 1173/5/7/10 [2013] CAT 18, [2013] EWCA Civ 1484.
95 *Iiyama Benelux Bv v Schott AG* [2016] 5 CMLR 15, (Ch); *Iiyama (Uk) Ltd v Samsung Electronics Co ltd* [2016] EWHC 1980 (Ch); [2016] 5 CMLR 16 and [2018] EWCA Civ 220; *Media-Saturn Holding GmbH v Toshiba Information systems*[2019] EWHC 1095 (Ch).
96 See the Civil Jurisdiction and Judgments (Amendment) (EU Exit) Regulations 2019, SI 2019/479.
97 See ibid, Explanatory Memorandum and Schedules 4 and 8 to the Civil Jurisdiction and Judgments Act 1982.
98 Regulation 864/2007 [2007] OJ L 299/40.
99 See the Law Applicable to Contractual Obligations and Non-Contractual Obligations (Amendment etc.) (EU Exit) Regulations 2019, SI 2019/834.

Ia Regulation have been lost, and pending the adoption of a satisfactory replacement mechanism, may reduce the attractiveness of the CAT (and High Court) as a forum for international litigation.[100]

Third, although the Antitrust Damages Directive will be treated as retained law, there are various aspects where subsequent changes may be introduced, with either damaging (limitation rules) or beneficial consequences (the rule on disclosure of leniency documentation) for private enforcement claimants. A potential impact of withdrawal is that the developing EU jurisprudence on substantive areas of EU law (e.g. in abuse of dominance) or in relation to effectiveness of the rights created under EU law will be limited in a UK context in claims under the Competition Act 1998 as a result of the revised interpretation s.60A, as discussed in greater detail in Chapter 2.

3.5 Concluding remarks

Over the last 20 years the courts in the UK have become increasingly attractive as a forum for international private litigation involving infringements of domestic and EU competition law rules.[101] This is partly as a result of the introduction of a range of legal, procedural and institutional mechanisms, including the specialist CAT. The UK's attractiveness as a forum reflects the experience of the established competition law plaintiff and defence bar in London, the availability of alternative forms of funding and incentives to litigate, and the experience and quality of the judiciary in competition law–related litigation. This includes the repeated and ongoing involvement of the Supreme Court in competition-related disputes. There have been a number of ways in which competition law claims have been encouraged and facilitated here: improved limitation and discovery provisions; provision for binding infringement decisions; a specialist court; a consumer collective redress scheme; and, subject to limitations, experimentation with creative forms of funding claims, notably through third-party funding.

The question is whether these existing and ongoing attractive features of the private enforcement framework in the UK will override the potential

---

100 While the courts may still exercise jurisdiction, there will be less certainty. Moreover, the mechanisms for recognition and enforcement across the EU Member States will not be as simple as under the Brussels Ia Regime, and there remains at this stage continued uncertainty regarding future arrangements, whether the UK will accede to the Lugano Convention or ratify the Hague Convention on the Recognition and Enforcement of Foreign Judgments in Civil or Commercial Matters, 2019.

101 B Rodger, 'Private Enforcement in the UK: Effective Redress for Consumers' in B Rodger, P Whelan and A MacCulloch (eds), *Twenty Years of UK Competition Law: A Retrospective* (Oxford University Press 2021) Chapter 12.

disadvantages associated with a legal context in which: EU law is treated as a foreign law; Commission decisions are no longer automatically binding on the courts; there are more complicated processes for recognition and enforcement judgments; and more indirect exposure to the guiding interpretation of the European Court of Justice for our domestic courts. There is widespread optimism that the strong bar, developing expertise and certainty in application of aspects of the rules by the judiciary, an increasingly (post-*Merricks*) effective collective damages recovery mechanism, and the availability of established third-party funders in the UK (effectively London), will help to overcome increasingly strong competition from other legal systems (e.g. the Netherlands) in attracting significant international competition litigation.

4　UK merger control[1]

4.1 Introduction

The impact of Brexit on competition law is likely to be most starkly felt in the context of merger control, as the EU-wide one-stop-shop is replaced by two parallel merger clearance regimes for businesses trading in the UK and the European Union (EU). Furthermore, in practical terms, merger control represents by far the greatest workload for competition authorities and competition law practitioners. This chapter will consider the potential impact of Brexit in relation to the processes of merger control in the UK. Merger control has particularly significant repercussions on the economy, and business mergers can enhance research and development, create efficiencies, merge complementary specialisms, and realise other forms of societal benefit.[2] Indeed, merger control is rarely about blocking controversial mergers and more commonly about facilitating beneficial arrangements, for instance joint ventures, by a speedy regulatory approval process that leaves parties certain as to the future viability and enforceability of their commercial arrangement. Accordingly, it is important for the parties to be aware of the system of regulatory approval required for any particular commercial arrangement, concentration, merger or takeover. The first aspect to be aware of is that the EU Merger Regulation (EUMR)[3] applies only to mergers with a Union dimension. Union dimension is a quantitative concept defined on the basis of the turnover of the parties to the merger, as defined in Article 1(2) of the Regulation. Moreover, Union

---

1 This chapter was co-authored with Dr David Reader, University of Newcastle Law School.
2 See for example K Cowling et al., *Mergers and Economic Performance* (Cambridge University Press 1980).
3 Council Regulation (EC) 139/2004 on the control of concentrations between undertakings (EU Merger Regulation) [2004] OJ L 24/1.

DOI: 10.4324/9781351105446-4

dimension mergers are, subject to further complicated provisions on potential referrals back to national competition authorities (NCAs),[4] only reviewable by the European Commission under a mandatory notification system under the EUMR – the so-called 'one-stop shop'. Such mergers fall within the exclusive competence of the European Commission[5] and cannot be reviewed by NCAs under national law.

In the UK context, this all changed as of 1 January 2021 when the transitional period following the UK's withdrawal from the EU ended. Of course, this does not affect any potential mergers or joint ventures which were not of a sufficient scale as to be caught by the EUMR thresholds. However, for Union dimension mergers which also trigger the UK merger control rules, the system of pre-emption in favour of the European Commission no longer applies and post-Brexit the parties to such mergers must seek regulatory approval from both the EU and the UK. Accordingly, this chapter will outline the system of merger control in the UK. Some mergers will now be considered under UK merger control law in addition to EU merger control, and it is important for the parties to be aware of the differences between the two. As with antitrust, the Trade and Cooperation Agreement entered into by the EU and the UK simply creates an obligation to maintain competition law that addresses anti-competitive mergers and acquisitions without any specific requirements or minimum rules.[6] The chapter will also address the likely foreseeable challenges and changes which may arise in light of – and in the wake of – UK withdrawal from the EU.[7] It is particularly important to understand the historical development of UK merger control to appreciate the contemporaneous post-Brexit debates about the future direction of travel of the UK regime.

The UK merger control regime under the Enterprise Act 2002 has attracted wide praise for the transparency and predictability it affords stakeholders through its robust competition-based assessment of mergers, carried out by a specialist independent competition authority. This stands in stark contrast to the framework that preceded it under the Fair Trading Act 1973,

---

4 See Articles 4 and 9 of the Regulation. See T Krajewska, 'Referrals under the New EC Merger Regulation: A UK Perspective' (2008) European Competition Law Review 279.

5 See *Gencor Ltd v Commission*, Case T-102/96, [1999] ECR II-753.

6 Trade and Cooperation Agreement between the European Union and the European Atomic Energy Community, of the one part, and the United Kingdom of Great Britain and Northern Ireland, of the other part. OJ[2020] L 444/14. Title XI, Article 2.2.

7 See also Brexit Competition Law Working Group, *Conclusions and Recommendations* (July 2017) paras 3.1–3.14.

which prescribed a broad public interest test.[8] Further legislative and procedural refinements over the past two decades have also afforded enhanced powers to the competition authority and delivered a more streamlined assessment process for merging parties. Nonetheless, the UK's continued use of a voluntary notification system is exceptional in comparison to most merger control systems,[9] and a limited role also endures for politicians to have the final say on mergers raising specific public interest concerns.

This chapter reflects on the evolution of UK merger control under the 2002 Act and contemplates its capacity to respond to contemporary challenges following UK withdrawal from the EU.

4.2 Merger control under the Enterprise Act 2002

4.2.1 A competition-based framework

In order to understand the implications of Brexit for businesses and legal advisers involved in takeovers and mergers, given the much broader scope of its post-Brexit application, it is necessary to undertake a relatively brief analysis of the UK merger control rules and processes. As of 20 June 2003, the 2002 Act replaced the merger control provisions of the Fair Trading Act 1973[10] based on the public interest and formally adopted an economic test for merger review, the substantial lessening of competition (SLC) test,[11] which still remains in place. The Act also sought to de-politicise the assessment process – and thereby make decision-making more predictable to businesses[12] – by removing the vast majority of decision-making powers from the Secretary of State and reassigning them to two independent competition authorities: the Office of Fair Trading (OFT) and the Competition Commission (CC). These agencies operated as part of a

---

8 S Wilks, *In the Public Interest: Competition Policy and the Monopolies and Mergers Commission* (Manchester University Press 1999) 226–227.

9 Only three countries within the OECD currently utilise a voluntary regime. OECD, 'Local Nexus and Jurisdictional Thresholds in Merger Control' (Background paper by the Secretariat, 10 March 2016), p. 9.

10 Fair Trading Act 1973, ss.84(1)(a)–(e). B Rodger, 'Reinforcing the Scottish "Ring-Fence": A Critique of UK Mergers Policy vis-a-vis the Scottish Economy' (1996) 17(2) European Competition Law Review 104, 112.

11 Specifically, the Enterprise Act 2002 Act prohibits any merger that 'has resulted, or may be expected to result, in a substantial lessening of competition' within the relevant market. See for example Enterprise Act 2002, ss.35(1)(b) and 36(1)(b), which express this wording in the context of Phase 2 investigations.

12 Department of Trade and Industry, *A World Class Competition Regime* (White Paper, CM 5233, 2001), paras 5.4 and A4.4.

two-phase merger review process, with the OFT performing an initial Phase 1 investigation and under a duty to refer any problematic mergers (i.e. those raising a realistic prospect of an SLC) to the CC for a further in-depth Phase 2 investigation.[13] Following its investigation, the CC would then publish a final Phase 2 decision on whether the case raised SLC concerns and, based on this, would exercise its powers to permit, prohibit or impose remedies on the merger. Of course, the roles of the OFT and the CC have now been subsumed within the Competition and Markets Authority (CMA) following the Enterprise and Regulatory Reform Act 2013. Moreover, decisions at all stages of the process by the CMA are subject to judicial review before a specialist judicial body, the Competition Appeal Tribunal (CAT).

Supplementing these institutional reforms under the 2002 Act was the UK's renewal of a voluntary system of notification, meaning there would be no legal requirement for parties to notify their merger to the OFT and no penalty for completing a merger that had not been issued with a clearance decision. These features collectively aimed to facilitate a regime that avoided undue burdens on businesses, while also renewing efforts to pursue a strict competition-based approach under the 2002 Act. The notable exception to this was the Act's retention of a residual power for the Secretary of State to intervene and assume the decision-making role in mergers that raise specific public interest concerns.[14] While 'national security' was the only public interest ground originally prescribed under the 2002 Act, this has since been joined by further grounds relating to media plurality and the presentation of news (in 2003), stability of the UK financial system (in 2008), and public health emergencies (in 2020). Both of these issues, the voluntary notification system and the potential for public interest concerns to affect merger control, may become particularly significant post-Brexit as discussed later.

4.2.2 The concept of a 'relevant merger situation'

An important factor in creating the one-stop shop for merger control and clearance when the UK was a part of the EU was the thresholds for application of the respective EU and UK rules. The merger control provisions of the 2002 Act only apply to transactions that have created – or are expected to create – a 'relevant merger situation'.[15] A relevant merger situation is

---

13 Enterprise Act 2002, ss.22(1)(b) and 33(1)(b), applying to completed and anticipated mergers respectively.
14 Enterprise Act 2002, s.42(2).
15 Enterprise Act 2002, ss.22(1)(a) and 33(1)(a) at Phase 1, and ss.35(1)(a) and 36(1)(a).

created where two or more enterprises have 'ceased to be distinct',[16] and *one* of two jurisdictional tests are satisfied; namely either (i) the UK turnover of the target/acquired firm exceeds £70 million (the turnover test), or (ii) the merger would result in the merging parties supplying (or, as the case may be, acquiring) 25% or more of a particular good or service in the UK (the share of supply test).[17] Furthermore, in cases where a merger had already been completed, a Phase 2 referral can be made within four months of (i) the merger being completed or (ii) the material facts of the merger entering the public domain (the four-month rule).[18] However, any merger with a Union dimension in accordance with the EU Merger Regulation, was effectively excluded from national, including UK, merger control.

4.2.3 *The residual public interest regime*

From its origins, the public interest test had been the 'cornerstone' of UK competition policy and merger control in particular, yet the 2002 Act had significantly limited the scope of its application and afforded it formal status as a mere 'exception' to the default competition-based test. Nonetheless, retaining some scope for political intervention on public interest grounds was seen as a necessity within the 2002 Act regime, aside from the named public interest grounds listed under s.58,[19] the Secretary of State was also afforded the power to add or remove a public interest ground from this list by virtue of s.58(3). Officially, this broad power was intended as a 'necessary safeguard' to provide flexibility in unforeseen circumstances,[20] so that 'very exceptional case[s] can be dealt with appropriately'.[21] The Secretary of State first exercised the powers contained in s.58(3) at the height of the 2007–2008 financial crisis, in order to introduce a new public interest ground for upholding 'the stability of the UK financial system'.[22] This new

16 ibid, s.23(1).
17 ibid, ss.23(1)(b) and 23(2)–(4). R Patel, 'BIS Reforms to the UK Merger Regime: An Opportunity Missed?' (2012) 11(2) Competition Law Journal 139, at 145–146.
18 ibid, s.24(1).
19 Which were 'national security' (s.58(1)) and, as introduced by the Communications Act 2003 shortly after the 2002 Act came into force, 'media plurality and presentation of news' (ss.58(2A)–(2C)).
20 HL Deb 15 October 2002, vol 639, col 801.
21 HL Deb 18 July 2002, vol 637, col 1466.
22 Enterprise Act 2002 (Specification of Additional Section 58 Consideration) Order 2008.

financial stability ground enabled the government to force through a 'rescue merger' involving Lloyds TSB's purchase of HBOS in 2008.[23]

As of June 2020, when 'public health emergencies' became the 2002 Act's fourth public interest ground (and the second to be introduced via the s.58(3) power),[24] the Secretary of State had issued a public interest intervention notice (PIIN) on only 20 occasions under the 2002 Act.[25] This enduring commitment to the competition-based approach comes in spite of repeated calls for successive governments to make greater use of the public interest powers in order to protect domestic firms from unwanted foreign takeovers, as discussed later.

4.3 The Enterprise and Regulatory Reform Act 2013 and fine-tuning the UK merger control regime

By 2011, the merger regime under the 2002 Act had independently been assessed as 'world class' for its legal and procedural effectiveness, in a report commissioned as part of a government consultation on competition reform.[26] The result of the consultation and subsequent legislative scrutiny was the 2013 Act, which introduced the most substantial changes to the 2002 Act regime to date. While the reforms were mainly of procedural refinement and strengthening, a significant institutional change was also realised.

On 1 April 2014, when the OFT and CC were abolished – or effectively merged – under the 2013 Act,[27] the newly established CMA inherited the Phase 1 and 2 roles of its predecessors. The CMA Board is now responsible for decision-making at Phase 1, while an independent Inquiry Group (comprising between three to five members selected from the CMA panel of independent experts) oversees the Phase 2 investigation and decision-making. The CMA has largely adopted the guidelines of its predecessors and has proceeded to update and publish new guidelines since its establishment.[28]

---

23 OFT, *Anticipated acquisition by Lloyds TSB plc of HBOS plc* (Report to BERR Secretary, 24 October 2008). See also A Stephan, 'Did Lloyds/HBOS Mark the Failure of an Enduring Economics-Based System of Merger Regulation?' (2011) 62(4) Northern Ireland Legal Quarterly 539, at 544.

24 Enterprise Act 2002 (Specification of Additional Section 58 Consideration) Order 2020.

25 There have been 12 interventions on national security grounds, 7 for media plurality, and 1 for financial stability.

26 The UK regime ranked second worldwide, behind the US; Department for Business, Innovation and Skills, *A Competition Regime for Growth: A Consultation on Options for Reform* (Consultation document, March 2011), para 1.5.

27 Enterprise and Regulatory Reform Act 2013, s.26.

28 See CMA, *Mergers: Guidance on the CMA's Jurisdiction and Procedure* (CMA2 revised December 2020).

Aside from the major institutional reforms, the broader workings of merger control were left relatively untouched by the 2013 Act.

The reform package for merger control constituted a fine-tuning of the existing merger control processes. A subsequent government review of the impact of the 2013 Act observed numerous positive outcomes, including predictability of decisions and the implementation of remedies. However, some commentators suggest opportunities for more radical change to the mergers regime were missed under the 2013 Act, especially concerning the viability of the UK's voluntary notification system.[29]

Despite aiming to minimise unnecessary red tape for merging parties, the voluntary notification system – and, more specifically, the lack of a mandatory system – has been described as a weakness of the UK regime.[30] Ultimately, however, the government decided that the 'most proportionate response' was to retain and strengthen the voluntary regime, as a mandatory system 'would increase costs to both business and the CMA'.[31]

While the fundamental traits of the 2002 Act survived the 2013 Act reform package, successive governments have demonstrated a desire to keep the UK merger control regime under review.[32] Emerging challenges continue to influence the agenda for reform, some of which are already influencing how the regime operates in practice. The government's 2019 *Competition Law Review* suggests further reforms are 'likely' to be needed for the CMA to effectively handle the larger number of multi-jurisdictional mergers in the post-Brexit era, which will be considered as part of the much-anticipated Competition Green Paper.[33] The regulation of unwanted foreign takeovers have also been discussed since the EU Referendum result, and recent revisions look set to be followed by more fundamental changes under the proposed National Security and Investment Bill. Moreover, the CMA's approach to mergers in the digital sector will undoubtedly remain on the policy agenda in the coming years.

29 See for example R Patel, 'BIS Reforms to the UK Merger Regime: An Opportunity Missed?' (2012) 11(2) Competition Law Journal 139, at 145–146; and K Gordon and C Hutton, 'An Opportunity Missed – The Proposed Reforms to the UK Competition Regime' (2012) 8(2) Competition Law International 49, at 49.

30 S Wilks, *In the Public Interest: Competition Policy and the Monopolies and Mergers Commission* (Manchester University Press 1999).

31 Department for Business, Innovation and Skills, *Growth, Competition and the Competition Regime: Government Response to the Consultation* (BIS 2012), para 5.8.

32 Department for Business, Innovation and Skills, *Options to Refine the UK Competition Regime: A Consultation* (May 2016), paras 27–31 and 41.

33 BEIS Competition Law Review, 2019, www.legislation.gov.uk/ukpga/2013/24/pdfs/ukp gaod_20130024_en.pdf (accessed 21 May 2021).

4.4 Post-Brexit challenges

4.4.1 Managing the post-Brexit caseload

The UK's departure from the EU removes the application of the 'one-stop shop' for merger clearances, previously available to transactions that meet both the UK and EU jurisdictional thresholds ('dual capture' mergers).[34] This will present a more expensive and procedurally onerous approval process for many businesses, and require the CMA to duplicate much of the work undertaken by the European Commission in merger investigations.[35] In practice, the additional filing requirement in the UK is unlikely to have a meaningful impact on 'mega-mergers' that already meet the jurisdictional thresholds of multiple regimes.[36] However, the prospect of other cross-border mergers facing two separate investigations (in the UK and the EU) may act to disincentivise merger activity in the UK, especially if the respective decisions of the CMA and European Commission prove to diverge on a regular basis.[37] As noted in Chapter 1, the exclusion of UK turnover from EU merger threshold calculations could mean that the dual scrutiny often involves the CMA and an EU national competition authority – in particular Ireland's Competition and Consumer Protection Commission.

One potential area for review post-Brexit is in relation to the thresholds for merger control in each of the two jurisdictions. At present the UK threshold is a turnover that exceeds £70 million or that the transaction results in the creation of (or increase in) a 25% or more combined share of sales or purchases in (or a substantial part of) the UK of goods or services.[38] By contrast, the threshold for the EUMR is where the combined aggregate worldwide turnover of the undertakings concerned is more than €5 billion and the aggregate European Community–wide turnover of at least two undertakings is more than €250 million (with additional thresholds for where turnover is focused on three or more Member States). It may be appropriate for the UK to increase its threshold slightly to help prioritise larger international merger

---

34 See for example P Johnson, 'Brexit: The Implications for EU and UK Merger Control' (2018) Competition Law Journal Brexit Special Online Edition 10–18; N Levy, 'Waiting for Brexit: Five Ways the CMA Could Improve UK Merger Control' [2020] 41(10) ECLR 487–499.

35 R Whish, 'Brexit and EU Competition Policy' (2016) 7(5) Journal of European Competition Law & Practice 297, at 297.

36 P Johnson, 'Brexit: The Implications for EU and UK Merger Control' (2018) Competition Law Journal Brexit Special Online Edition 10–18.

37 M Rees and C Flynn, 'Effect of a British Exit from the EU on Competition Law Enforcement in the UK' (2015) 21(3) International Trade Law and Regulation 67, at 68.

38 CMA, revised supra n 28, paras 4.56–4.63.

clearance, although this appears to run counter to more recent developments in the field. Moreover, it may also be appropriate for the EU to consider whether it should reduce its thresholds to reflect the reduced size of EU markets following the withdrawal of the UK's economy from the single market.

It should be noted at this stage that there are four areas for potential divergence where the EU and UK merger regimes apply in parallel. The first concerns the differing notification requirements under the EUMR and the 2002 Act, with the former requiring mandatory prior notification of any qualifying concentration. A second linked issue concerns the different merger control timetables under the two systems, although both include two phases of investigation. Third is a substantive issue related to the test for assessing mergers – here the two competition tests are ostensibly different: 'the significant impediment to effective competition' (SIEC) test under the EUMR and the SLC test under the 2002 Act. Whilst both competition-based tests will result in broadly similar assessment processes and outcomes in both jurisdictions, there is scope for divergence, notably in relation to the potential application of the subsidiary structural dominance test under the EUMR compatibility test formulation. A fourth related issue concerns the scope and potential application of the subsidiary public interest regime under the 2002 Act to a merger assessed only under the SIEC competition test at the EU level, as discussed further later.

The CMA has proceeded to invest in the appointment of new staff, many of whom will be assigned to reviewing an estimated 50 additional Phase 1 cases a year.[39] In an effort to manage this extra workload and mitigate the effects on the CMA's resources, it has been suggested that policymakers – and the CMA itself – may invoke the expertise of sector regulators on a more routine basis in order to conduct 'quick' assessments of mergers taking place in particular markets.[40] Evidently, however, more drastic change is necessary if the CMA is to effectively manage the resources it allocates to merger reviews, despite the increase in its budget and staffing. The government has itself conceded that the increased responsibility on the CMA to deal with large-scale mergers suggests 'a need for wider reform' and, in particular, a requirement to 'work in parallel with other jurisdictions, including the EU, [which] may require changes to current procedures' under the 2002 Act.[41]

---

39 B Thompson, 'UK Competition Watchdog Braced for Jump in Workload after Brexit' *The Financial Times* (London, 5 February 2019) www.ft.com/content/9fd79e72-12a7-11e9-a5 81-4ff78404524e (accessed 1 September 2020).

40 P Johnson, 'Brexit: The Implications for EU and UK Merger Control' (2018) Competition Law Journal Brexit Special Online Edition 10–18.

41 Department for Business, Energy & Industrial Policy, *Competition Law Review: Post Implementation Review of Statutory Changes in the Enterprise Regulatory Reform Act*

As discussed in Chapter 1, Section 1.2 of this volume, close cooperation between the two authorities will be important in creating more consistency and alignment between assessment outcomes.[42] Alternatively, some have suggested a 'partial remedy' would be for the UK to adopt a review timetable that aligns more closely to the EUMR's,[43] or a 'more complete solution' of adopting a system of mandatory notification that would allow both the CMA and European Commission to start their investigatory clocks at similar times.[44] In an open letter to the Secretary of State in 2019, the then chairman of the CMA, Lord Tyrie, called for a mandatory notification regime and standstill obligations for mergers above a certain threshold, in place of the existing interim measures under the voluntary regime.[45] While the UK's voluntary notification system was passionately defended during consultations leading up to the 2013 Act, Brexit undoubtedly moves the goalposts on the debate. The informality of the UK notification system provides the CMA with a greater degree of freedom over the type and, in turn, number of cases it calls in,[46] but this freedom does not extend to disregarding any merger it deems to have a realistic potential of resulting in an SLC. Here, there is a fine balance to be struck between the resources allocated to the CMA's mergers intelligence function and to its Phase 1 case teams; adequate investment in the former remains critical for as long as the UK continues to endorse a system of voluntary notification. An unfortunate reality is that, short of infinite time and resources, the CMA's procedural aims (of efficiently identifying and reviewing potentially harmful mergers) may need to take priority over substantive norms (e.g. a business-friendly approach to notification, a fresh pair of eyes at Phase 2, etc.).

2013 (2019).

42 N Parr and C Hammon, 'UK Merger Control at a Crossroads' (2017) 16(1) Competition Law 13.

43 LM Davison, 'Envisaging the Post-Brexit Landscape: An Articulation of the Likely Changes to the EU-UK Competition Policy Relationship' (2018) 39 Liverpool Law Review 99, at 115.

44 ibid, 115–116.

45 Letter from Lord Tyrie to the Secretary of State for Business, Energy and Industrial Strategy (21 February 2019). Lord Tyrie's letter was previously mentioned in Chapter 2, Section 2.4 of this volume.

46 P Roth, 'Competition Law and Brexit: The Challenges Ahead' (2017) 16(1) Competition Law 5, at 7.

4.4.2 The public interest regime and nationalist protectionism

Outside the jurisdiction of the EUMR, the UK government will also have greater freedom to intervene in large cross-border mergers on public interest grounds. Prior to Brexit, the government would have to request jurisdiction to review the public interest element of an EU-level merger under Article 21(4) EUMR. This provision affords Member States the opportunity to assume competence over mergers that raise 'legitimate national interest' concerns, which include public security, media plurality and prudential rules (as part of a non-exhaustive list). Significantly, the European Commission will only consider granting an Article 21(4) request if the merger itself does not arouse suspicion of creating a significant impediment to effective competition (SIEC).[47] Together with the Commission applying a traditionally narrow interpretation to what constitutes a 'legitimate national interest',[48] the application of Article 21(4) has previously acted to temper the UK's ability to intervene in large-scale European mergers involving 'crown jewel' firms based in the UK.[49]

While the narrow scope of Article 21(4) proved a hindrance to the UK's pursuit of public interest interventions, it also provided 'an important safeguard against protectionism and undue political intervention',[50] to which a post-Brexit UK regime is no longer subject. Brexit opens up opportunities for the UK to use its public interest powers under the 2002 Act to block (or extract undertakings from) mergers that have been approved by the European Commission and the opportunity for the UK to permit (on public interest grounds) a merger that the European Commission has blocked (on competition grounds), assuming that the EU aspects of the merger can be 'carved-out of the wider transaction'.[51] The shackles of the EUMR are being removed at a time when calls for economic protectionism in relation to foreign investments and takeovers are becoming increasingly audible.[52]

---

47 European Commission, 'Community Merger Control Law' (1990) Bulletin of the European Communities, Supplement 2/90, 24.

48 M Harker, 'Cross-Border Mergers in the EU: The Commission v the Member States' (2007) 3(2) ECJ 503.

49 For example Pfizer's failed approach for AstraZeneca reportedly saw the Commission ready to reject an Article 21(4) request from the UK, which was seeking to protect the UK science base. D Reader, 'Pfizer/AstraZeneca and the Public Interest: Do UK Foreign Takeover Proposals Prescribe an Effective Remedy?' (2014) 10(1) CPI Antitrust Chronicle.

50 B Lyons, D Reader and A Stephan, 'UK Competition Policy Post-Brexit: Taking Back Control while Resisting Siren Calls' (2017) 5(3) Journal of Antitrust Enforcement 347, at 356.

51 See N Parr and C Hammon, 'UK Merger Control at a Crossroads' (2017) 16(1) Competition Law Journal 13.

52 A Jones and J Davies, 'Merger Control and the Public Interest: Balancing EU and National Law in the Protectionist Debate' (2014) 10(3) European Competition Journal 453, at 492.

With greater freedom to intervene and to propose new public interest grounds under s.58(3) of the 2002 Act, the Secretary of State may well come under pressure to exercise these powers when a foreign bidder (or an unpopular domestic bidder) seeks to acquire a popular or lucrative domestic firm. Moreover, s.58(3) requires only secondary legislative approval for new public interest grounds to be enacted, denying Parliament the opportunity to rigorously scrutinise provisions that – collectively – stand to have a significant impact on the perceived certainty and transparency of the merger regime.

As early as 2018, the government had begun to legislate for greater powers to intervene in mergers that raise national security concerns,[53] namely by amending the share of supply test and lowering the turnover test threshold from £70m to £1m for mergers involved in (i) the dual use and military use sector; (ii) parts of the advanced technology sector; and – as of July 2020 – (iii) artificial intelligence, (iv) cryptographic authentication, and (v) advanced materials.[54] The scope of these provisions is potentially vast, capable of capturing a hundred or more additional cases each year, by government estimates.[55] Given the relevance of these sectors and technologies to the government's Industrial Strategy, in which the Business Secretary is tasked with targeting companies to invest in specific UK sectors,[56] an evident conflict of interest arises.

Given the prevalent role that national security review is set to play in the post-Brexit era, it is also critical that the concept of 'national security' does not lose the specific meaning intended for it by the drafters of the 2002 Act, as was close to being the case in *Melrose/GKN*.[57] The definition that the 2002 Act ascribes to 'national security' is notably narrower than that of many other developed countries. Under the 2002 Act, there is no scope for the Business Secretary to consider industrial policy concerns

---

53 D Reader, 'Extending "National Security" in Merger Control and Investment: A Good Deal for the UK?' (2018) 14(1) Competition Law International 35.

54 Enterprise Act 2002, s.23A (as amended).

55 The government estimated that 'fewer than 100 transactions per year' would be captured by the initial reforms, while it expects an 'additional 16 cases' to arise from the 2020 reforms. See Department for Business, Energy and Industrial Strategy, *National Security and Infrastructure Investment Review* (Green Paper, 2017), para 154; and HL Secondary Legislative Scrutiny Committee, *21st Report of Session 2019-21* (HL Paper 96, 9 July 2020), para 6.

56 HM Government, 'Industrial Strategy: Building a Britain Fit for the Future' (White Paper, Cm 9528, 2017) 190.

57 D Reader, 'Why "National Security" Concerns Are Unlikely to Impede the Melrose/GKN Takeover' (*Competition Policy Blog*, 8 February 2018) https://competitionpolicy.word press.com/2018/02/08/why-national-security-concerns-are-unlikely-to-impede-the-melros e-gkn-takeover (accessed 1 September 2020).

when reviewing a merger on national security grounds. While Parliament had initially struggled to identify a precise definition for 'national security' in debates around the Enterprise Bill,[58] Hansard debate reveals the definition to be closely aligned to protecting the personal safety and security of citizens,[59] rather than any form of economic security. Lord Sainsbury confirmed this by remarking that any intervention on the grounds of 'economic security' (to protect, for example, an asset that is 'essential to large parts of the British economy') would require the Secretary of State to propose a new public interest ground using their power under (what is now) s.58(3).[60]

Further fundamental reform is set out in the National Security and Investment Bill. This bill introduces a new regime for monitoring inward investment on national security grounds and requires any purchase that amounts to more than 15% of the value of any company in one of 17 key industrial sectors to be notified to a new body called the Investment and Security Unit (ISU). When the ISU has concerns, the government has the power to block the transaction without any assessment by the CMA as to the competition merits of the case. John Fingleton, the former head of the OFT, has warned that it 'will encourage any vested interest that does not like the look of a deal to lobby politicians to call it in for investigation on national security grounds'.[61] While the very existence of a national security review procedure may have the effect of reducing foreign investment into the UK, an overtly expansive and aggressive review procedure could inflict irreputable damage on the UK's ability to attract 'welcome' investment, as well as restricting that which is unwanted.[62]

4.4.3 The challenge presented by digital mergers

Understanding and assessing the dynamic theories of harm associated with mergers in the digital sector is among the hottest topics for any competition

---

58 Enterprise HC Bill (2001–02) 115. The bill's sponsor commented that 'national security is like an elephant: one knows it when one sees it'; Enterprise Bill Deb 30 April 2002, col 356.

59 S.58(2) explicitly acknowledges that 'national security' includes 'public security' within the meaning of Article 21(4) EU Merger Regulation (which has been interpreted as relating to mergers with connections or contractual ties to the military or to the maintenance of public health).

60 HL Deb 18 July 2002, vol 637, col 1490.

61 J Fingleton, 'Britain Must Rethink Its "National Security" Law' *The Financial Times* (23 January 2021).

62 J Fingleton, 'Mergers and the Public Interest: A Wolf in Sheep's Clothing?' (Fingleton Associates, 16 October 2018) https://fingleton.com/news/mergers-and-the-public-interest -a-wolf-in-sheeps-clothing (accessed 1 August 2020).

authority at present. One of the main theories relates to 'killer acquisitions',[63] where a large digital firm purchases a 'younger', smaller start-up firm that has yet to realise its potential in the market, with the purpose of removing it as a potential future competitor.[64] The effect is an overall loss of innovation (and incentives to innovate) in a highly concentrated market, meaning the digital economy fails to reach its full potential.[65]

In the UK, the policy debate in this area has been largely shaped by two seminal reports published in 2019; the government-commissioned *Report of the Digital Competition Expert Panel* (hereafter, 'the Furman Report'),[66] and the CMA-commissioned Lear Report.[67] Both reports were critical of what they observed as underenforcement of mergers in digital markets by the UK competition authorities. The Furman Report suggested that 'false negative' approvals may have taken place as a result of no digital mergers being blocked under the 2002 Act,[68] and the Lear Report indicated a tendency of the authorities to err towards underenforcement in order to avoid overenforcement.[69] The Lear Report also describes significant merger and acquisition M&A activity among the Big Tech players and how they most often (in 60% of mergers) acquire young firms of four years old or less.[70]

Each report makes its own recommendations to detect harmful mergers in the sector and to improve overall enforcement. Among the most prominent of the Furman proposals was to legislate in order to introduce a 'balance of harms' test for digital mergers under the 2002 Act, which would require the CMA to take into account 'the scale as well as the likelihood of harm in merger cases involving potential competition and harm to innovation'.[71] Believing the traditional SLC test to present too high a threshold for the CMA to effectively consider dynamic theories of harm, the balance of harms approach 'would mean mergers being blocked when they are expected to do more harm than good'. The Lear Report, on the other

---

63 For an insightful overview, see C Pike, 'Start-Ups, Killer Acquisitions and Merger Control' (2020) OECD Background Note DAF/COMP(2020)5. See also K Desai, 'Changes for the Digital Economy – Merger Control' (2019) 3(2) CoRe 122, at 126.

64 See for example K Desai, 'Changes for the Digital Economy – Merger Control' (2019) 3(2) CoRe 122.

65 ibid, 127.

66 Digital Competition Expert Panel, 'Unlocking Digital Competition' (Independent report, HM Treasury 2019).

67 Lear, *Ex-post Assessment of Merger Control Decisions in Digital Markets: Final Report* (Independent report prepared for the CMA, May 2019).

68 Furman Report, para 3.43.

69 Lear Report, para I.148.

70 ibid, para I.150.

71 Furman Report, 10.

hand, recommended placing greater emphasis on the value of transactions in an effort to screen for problematic deals; where the price paid by the acquiring firm is unexplainably high for a young firm, the motives of the acquirer should be questioned to determine whether the merger is intended to kill off emerging competition.[72]

In response to the Furman and Lear Reports, the chief executive of the CMA initially claimed that the authority's merger control toolkit was 'fit-for-purpose' in terms of addressing concerns related to killer acquisitions in the digital sector.[73] He did, however, appreciate a need for the CMA to rebalance its approach to enforcement and, potentially, to subject powerful companies to greater scrutiny, especially where entry barriers are high and competition is essentially 'for' the market rather than 'within' it. A year later, while reaffirming its belief that the current merger regime is 'largely fit-for-purpose', the CMA confirmed that it was 'considering the need for legislative changes' to ensure it has the right tools to prevent consumers being harmed by digital mergers.[74] In October 2020, the Chief Executive announced that the CMA was considering advising the government to create a 'parallel merger regime' for digital mergers that would potentially be subject to mandatory notification and a lower standard of proof under the SLC test.[75] It was anticipated that this special parallel regime 'could also accommodate a separate assessment of non-competition concerns such as data protection'.[76] This parallel regime was instituted in April 2021, with a new Digital Markets Unit (DMU) within the CMA tasked with enforcing a statutory code of conduct for digital platforms that possess 'strategic market status'.[77] The DMU derives significant enforcement powers from the code, including 'powers to suspend, block and reverse the decisions of tech giants' as well as powers to impose compliance orders and fines for non-compliance.[78]

---

72 Lear Report, para I.154.
73 A Coscelli, 'Competition in the Digital Age: Reflecting on Digital Merger Investigations' (OECD/G7 Conference on Competition and the Digital Economy, Paris, 3 June 2019).
74 CMA, *Online Platforms and Digital Advertising Market Study: Final Report* (1 July 2020), para 10.31.
75 It is anticipated that this regime would apply to firms who are deemed to have 'strategic market status'. Andrea Coscelli, 'Digital Markets: Using Our Existing Tools and Emerging Thoughts on a New Regime' (Fordham Competition Law Institute 47th Annual Conference on International Antitrust Law and Policy, Virtual Conference, 9 October 2020).
76 ibid.
77 HM Government, 'New Competition Regime for Tech Giants to Give Consumers More Choice and Control over Their Data, and Ensure Businesses Are Fairly Treated' (Press release, 27 November 2020).
78 ibid.

The introduction of the DMU will empower the CMA to address the challenge of digital mergers under a prescriptive code that is reinforced by enhanced enforcement powers. The approach to enforcement will also require more 'imagination' going forward,[79] including through further engagement with the non-price effects of mergers.[80] However, some of this refinement risks stretching the 2002 Act provisions beyond their means in ways that may not be readily accommodated under the new statutory code. For example, while the SLC test allows for the consideration of dynamic competition, this does not tie in well with the 'robust' measures that competition authorities usually deploy.[81] A substantive test akin to the 'balance of harms' test proposed by the Digital Competition Expert Panel, or a lower evidential threshold to allow the CMA to accept more uncertainty when considering counterfactuals as proposed by the Lear Report, may offer a more workable approach. Equally, a value-based jurisdictional test would improve the chances of capturing killer acquisitions, especially given these young firms are far less likely to meet the turnover or share of supply thresholds under the 2002 Act.[82] The prospect of non-competition concerns being considered within a parallel merger regime is perhaps the most revolutionary of these proposals. Any departure from the 2002 Act's strict competition-based approach would first require a meticulous impact assessment, but there is merit in affording the CMA the ability to holistically address merger-specific issues of privacy and data protection within a limited range of merger cases. It is certainly clear that – post-Brexit – the CMA will be dedicating considerable time and resources in developing its merger and other enforcement tools to deal with potentially anti-competitive aspects of the digital economy.

4.5 Concluding remarks

Tailored adjustments to the 2002 Act have delivered a merger control regime that, for the most part, provides a transparent, consistent and business-friendly review process. It is therefore well placed to apply to all merger situations that trigger UK merger regulation, alongside parallel procedures by the European Commission, or an EU NCA, in relation to the

---

79 P Roth, 'The Continual Evolution of Competition Law' (2019) 7(1) Journal of Antitrust Enforcement 6, at 23.
80 P Wantoch et al., 'Non-Price Effects of Mergers' (2019) 18(2) Competition Law Journal 73.
81 P Roth, 'The Continual Evolution of Competition Law' (2019) 7(1) Journal of Antitrust Enforcement 6, at 23.
82 ibid, 24.

same transactions. As already discussed in Chapter 1, merger control is also likely to be an area where cooperation between the UK and EU continues to be strong – especially given the consensual nature of merger cases on the part of the undertakings. The combination of cooperation and the similar nature of the merger tests applied by the two jurisdictions make diverging outcomes unlikely. Indeed, in April 2021 the CMA issued a joint statement with other leading competition authorities calling for more 'rigorous and effective merger enforcement'.[83]

The more pressing questions that arise from Brexit relate to the CMA's approach to digital mergers and the possible scope for greater interventions on public interest grounds such as national security and in dealing with digital markets. The CMA has been confident of tailoring its approach to digital mergers using its existing toolkit, but it remains to be seen whether the SLC test is able to accommodate fully dynamic theories of harm under a more 'imaginative' approach, or whether a new substantive test or a lower standard of proof for digital mergers should be adopted.

As a consequence of Brexit and a general rise in nationalist sentiment, the Secretary of State now risks being put under greater pressure to intervene in mergers – and, in particular, foreign takeovers – on public interest grounds and to introduce new public interest grounds using the s.58(3) power. While objectively legitimate interests may well be pursued under this power,[84] expanding the scope and application of the public interest exceptions is a slippery slope and, once the Secretary of State blocks or permits one merger, it establishes an expectation that other interventions are also justifiable. The National Security and Investment Bill potentially poses an even greater danger in this respect, as it appears to create the possibility of mergers being blocked on national security grounds without any advice having been taken from the CMA.

The CMA's role is critical and, going forward, funding and resource management will greatly influence the early performance of UK merger control in the post-Brexit era. Further procedural refinements (e.g. converging closer to the EUMR review timetable) may well be necessary to aid the CMA's transition towards a significantly larger caseload, and calls to depart from the voluntary notification system should remain on the back-burner until the extent of the CMA's task is fully appreciated.

---

83   Policy Paper: Joint statement on merger control enforcement by the Competition and Markets Authority (CMA), Australian Competition and Consumer Commission (ACCC) and Bundeskartellamt.

84   Holmes, for example, advocates the introduction of 'sustainability and climate change' as a named public interest ground. S Holmes, 'Climate Change, Sustainability and Competition Law in the UK' (2020) 41(8) European Competition Law Rreview 384, at 392.

5   State aid

This chapter deals with perhaps the most contentious of competition policy areas in the Brexit process – the EU's rules on State aid (or 'subsidy control') and the question of how the UK should be bound by them as part of its post-Brexit trading relationship with the EU. As State aid is often treated as a separate discipline to competition law, this chapter begins with an outline of how State aid rules work and how the European Commission determines whether aid is unlawful. As was noted in Chapter 1, the Commission has exclusive competence to review and approve State aid as part of the EU's notification regime. At the end of the transition period, the UK had no domestic system of subsidy control in place, even though this had been strongly recommended within the UK and was a fundamental EU demand (that the UK ended up conceding). Indeed, the obligations created by the EU–UK Trade and Cooperation Agreement (TCA) are far more detailed and binding than the provisions on antitrust and mergers. In critically analysing the impact of Brexit on UK subsidy control, the chapter will consider whether the UK has been a net beneficiary of State aid rules, how these rules compare to World Trade Organization (WTO) rules on subsidies, how subsidies are dealt with by Free Trade Agreements, whether a national system of subsidy control was desirable (including the role of an independent authority) and an analysis of the obligations created by the TCA.

5.1 What is State aid and when is it unlawful?

State aid is where a public authority (whether at a national or regional level) confers any advantage to a business on a selective basis, that is not on commercial terms and which may affect cross-border trade or investment within the European Union (EU). State aid can take a number of different forms, but typically exists in the shape of subsidies and tax concessions. It

DOI: 10.4324/9781351105446-5

is governed in EU law by Article 107 of the Treaty on the Functioning of the European Union (TFEU), which states:

> Save as otherwise provided in this Treaty, any aid granted by a Member State or through State resources in any form whatsoever which *distorts or threatens to distort competition by favouring certain undertakings or the production of certain goods* shall, in so far as it affects trade between Member States, be incompatible with the common market. [emphasis added]

There are lawful forms of State aid that can be awarded, as discussed later, and Article 107 is designed to only prevent Member States from engaging in the kind of wasteful subsidy competition that has historically been a characteristic of international trade disputes. In a competition context, the risk is that firms in other Member States are disadvantaged if the distortive aid attracts investment that would otherwise have gone to them, or allows the subsidised firm to invest more, or remain in business when it would otherwise close down. Where it is selective, it also risks sparking a subsidy war between governments seeking to protect their own national champions. It is notable that in the US, where there is no domestic subsidy control regime, cities and regions are often pitted against each other by firms seeking financial incentives to move factories and headquarters.[1] Having some form of subsidy control also protects the economy from political short-termism and excessive business lobbying. For example, even if a government understands the wasteful nature of the aid itself, they might still consider it to be worthwhile if it helps secure them a further term in office.[2]

5.1.1 Why are some forms of subsidy harmful?

There are WTO rules on subsidies (discussed later) that have strong parallels with EU State aid law. These exist because in an international context, an export subsidy will be distortive by increasing the quantity of exports and reducing the domestic price of that product in other countries, while maintaining a higher price domestically.[3] This has a very similar effect to a restriction of competition in an antitrust or merger context. The

---

1 See, for example, 'Amazon's HQ2 Spectacle Isn't Just Shameful – It Should Be Illegal' *The Atlantic* (12 November 2018).
2 M Dewatripont and P Seabright, 'Wasteful Public Spending and State Aid Control' (2006) 4(2–3) Journal of the European Economic Association 513–522.
3 On the effects of export subsidies, see S Suranovic, *International Economics: Theory and Policy* (Saylor Foundation, 2012) Chapter 7.

export subsidy will reduce consumer surplus and raise producer surplus in the country issuing the export ban, while harming the ability of foreign producers to compete. The overall effect of an export subsidy (of any size) is therefore to reduce world supply of the product and cause a loss of welfare overall, in the same way that a monopoly or a cartel would.[4] Where an importing country reacts to the export subsidy with a countervailing duty, prices will normally revert back to their free trade levels and the net effect will be a transfer of income from the export country's government to the import country's government.[5]

The forms of subsidies that are generally beneficial are those designed to deal with a market failure, such as a positive externality. This is where the benefits associated with producing and consuming a product are not fully taken into account by the producer or the consumer. For example, consumers may be reluctant to switch to renewable sources of energy if the cost is significantly higher than sources that are predominantly reliant on fossil fuels. Therefore, a subsidy on green energy or on electric cars helps push consumption to a socially optimal level, by making them more affordable to consumers.[6] Similarly, subsidy schemes introduced during the Covid crisis were beneficial in preventing otherwise healthy businesses from going bankrupt or dismissing their staff. Other examples of subsidies aimed at providing socially beneficial outcomes that are not delivered by the free market include access to broadband in rural areas, a nationwide postal service, regional television services and public transport.[7] Whereas addressing a market failure is an efficiency rationale for State aid, some of the aforementioned examples are not market failures per se, but rather to do with equity, or market outcomes that are not socially or politically acceptable. The challenge from a policy perspective is how to balance these beneficial uses of State aid, against any distorting effect on competition or external harm caused to consumers or competitors in other Member States.

The harm to competition mainly comes down to loss of efficiency. It is in the interest of consumers and the wider economy for goods and services to be produced as efficiently as possible, which does not necessarily mean

4 ibid, 7.17. JA Brander and BJ Spencer, 'Export Subsidies and International Market Share Rivalry' (1985) 18 Journal of International Economics 83–100.
5 ibid, 7.18.
6 WTO, World Trade Report 2006, Chapter II, pp. 61–63, www.wto.org/english/res_e/booksp _e/anrep_e/wtr06-2c_e.pdf (accessed 18 August 2020).
7 J Haucap and U Schwalbe, 'Economic Principles of State Aid Control' (April 2011) Dusseldorf Institute for Competition Economics, Discussion Paper No. 17, p. 5, pointing out that recognition of the benefits of subsidies goes back some way: Pigou, *The Economics of Welfare* (Macmillan 1920).

as cheaply as possible, as quality can be a key driver of competition. State aid can distort this competitive pressure by protecting inefficient or failing firms, discouraging innovation and possibly causing a competitor of the firm receiving assistance to exit the market.[8] Bankruptcy is necessary for the economy to work efficiently – if demand for a product or service is dropping, then the least efficient firm may fold. Although this results in fewer competitors, it may mean the level of efficiency in the market increases as a result, outweighing any loss of competition. State aid may artificially protect the least efficient firm from leaving the market in this way.[9]

Aid will also be wasteful when it goes to an investment that would have happened anyway, as this benefits shareholders at the expense of the taxpayer. In economic terms, this reflects the poor opportunity cost of State aid, as the money could have been put to more socially beneficial good. While State aid can legitimately be used to redress inequality within the EU, the fact richer Member States and regions have deeper pockets can compound the opposite effect – awarding aid that widens regional disparities in wealth.[10] This highlights further problems associated with State aid: it is susceptible to lobbying and political short-termism, as described earlier.[11] Lobbying is particularly effective where the government only has partial information about an industry or a particular firm.

The use of State aid in this way can also constitute a massive waste of public money, which could otherwise have been put to better use. This is especially so when two governments are subsidising their key competitors in a certain market or engage in retaliatory measures, as any benefit of the subsidy is essentially cancelled out.[12] However, this view of State aid is not shared by all jurisdictions. In the US, for example, a more laissez-faire approach is taken to domestic subsidies, as alluded to earlier, and Congress rarely takes action to stop them at the State level and has very limited powers to do so.[13] It has also been suggested that the WTO Agreement

---

8 See Department for Business, Innovation & Skills, *The State aid Manual* (July 2015) at 1.1.

9 MAB Ferruz and P Nicolaides, 'The Economics of State Aid for the Rescue and Restructuring of Firms in Difficulty: Theoretical Considerations, Empirical Analysis and Proposals for Reform' (2013) Bruges European Economic Research Papers 27/2013.

10 M Morris and T Kibasi, *State Aid Rules and Brexit* (January 2019) Institute for Public Policy Research, p. 7.

11 C Buelens et al., 'The Economic Analysis of State Aid: Some Open Questions' (September 2007) 286 European Economy Economic Papers 8.

12 S Lehner and R Meiklejohn, 'Fair Competition in the Internal Market: Community State Aid Policy' (1991) European Economy No. 48, European Commission.

13 See discussion in AO Sykes, 'The Questionable Case for Subsidies Regulation: A Comparative Perspective' (2010) 2(2) Journal of Legal Analysis 474–523; C Buelens

on Subsidies and Countervailing Measures (discussed later) is one of the few international agreements with no preamble at all, because the drafters decided that it would be impossible to agree to its objectives and purpose.[14]

5.1.2 How do EU State aid rules work?

Not all public funding is State aid under EU law. In order for it to be covered by Article 107, it must favour certain undertakings or the production of certain goods (i.e. not available to everyone), it must distort or threaten to distort competition and it must affect trade between Member States. It is also important to point out that the beneficiary of the aid does not need to be a private business. The normal meaning of 'undertaking' in competition law applies, meaning that it can include any public entity engaged in economic activity.

The TFEU and supporting regulations, guidelines and case law provide a guide as to the forms of State aid that are permissible – these are for reasons of general economic development. For example, paragraphs 2 and 3 of Article 107 state that:

2. The following shall be compatible with the internal market:
   (a) aid having a social character, granted to individual consumers, provided that such aid is granted without discrimination related to the origin of the products concerned;
   (b) aid to make good the damage caused by natural disasters or exceptional occurrences;
   (c) aid granted to the economy of certain areas of the Federal Republic of Germany affected by the division of Germany, in so far as such aid is required in order to compensate for the economic disadvantages caused by that division. Five years after the entry into force of the Treaty of Lisbon, the Council, acting on a proposal from the Commission, may adopt a decision repealing this point.
3. The following may be considered to be compatible with the internal market:
   (a) aid to promote the economic development of areas where the standard of living is abnormally low or where there is serious

---

et al., 'The Economic Analysis of State Aid: Some Open Questions' (September 2007) 286 European Economy Economic Papers 2.

14 A Biondi, 'Brexit and State Aid Control: Four Quartets' (2018) Competition Law Journal, 17(2), 3–12, at 7, citing M Cartland et al., 'Is Something Wrong in the WTO Dispute Settlement?' (2012) 46(5) Journal of World Trade 979, at 992.

> underemployment, and of the regions referred to in Article 349, in view of their structural, economic and social situation;
>
> (b) aid to promote the execution of an important project of common European interest or to remedy a serious disturbance in the economy of a Member State;
>
> (c) aid to facilitate the development of certain economic activities or of certain economic areas, where such aid does not adversely affect trading conditions to an extent contrary to the common interest;
>
> (d) aid to promote culture and heritage conservation where such aid does not affect trading conditions and competition in the Union to an extent that is contrary to the common interest;
>
> (e) such other categories of aid as may be specified by decision of the Council on a proposal from the Commission.

State aid is subject to a pre-notification procedure, whereby the European Commission can either approve or decline it. In examining the aid, the Commission undertakes a balancing test, to see if the benefits (in terms of contributing to an objective of EU interest) outweigh the costs (in terms of a distortion of competition and trade). In doing so they will have regard to whether it is an appropriate instrument (could another policy tool have been used to address the problem?), whether there is an incentive effect (i.e. checking that the counterfactual is not that the desired outcome would have happened anyway), whether the aid is proportionate and whether the distortions of competition are limited (i.e. the overall balance).[15] One of the reasons it is in the best interests of governments to give careful consideration and planning to aid is that it is permissible for the Commission to start with a presumption that the aid distorts or threatens to distort competition.[16]

Where State aid is granted without being notified to the Commission, it is treated as illegal until it is determined as either being compatible or incompatible with the treaty. It will usually be suspended until its compatibility can be determined and the consequences of it being found incompatible are severe. The Commission can rule that the aid must be paid back in full with interest and Member States must recover the illegal aid even if it means a recipient company will go bankrupt. State aid rules

---

15 For articulations of the balancing test, see European Commission, *State Aid Action Plan, Less and Better Targeted State Aid: A Roadmap for State Aid Reform 2005 to 2009* (2005) Competition Policy Newsletter 2; Department for Business, Innovation & Skills, *The State Aid Manual* (July 2015) at 8.19–20.

16 Case 730/79 *Philip Morris v Commission*.

also empower private parties, in that a competitor not benefiting from the aid can take action to recover damages from both the awarding Member State government and the recipients of the aid, although such actions are very rare. This will be in addition to the recovery of the aid itself by the Member State.

To reduce the burden on both Member States and the Commission, there is a General Block Exemption Regulation, which declares certain categories of aid as compatible and discharges the obligation on Member States to use the notification procedure.[17] This block exemption is focused on aid that is unlikely to cause significant distortions of competition, such as support for small- and medium-sized businesses, and also aid focused on innovation, dealing with natural disasters, key infrastructure, and the conservation of cultural assets. There is also a *de minimis* threshold of €200,000 per undertaking over a three-year period.[18]

A guiding principle for what is not State aid is known as the Market Economy Operator (MEO) principle. The question is 'whether, in similar circumstances, a private investor of a comparable size operating in normal conditions of a market economy could have been prompted to make the investment in question'.[19] It is not considered State aid where the beneficiary is essentially getting funding on the same terms that would be available to it from the market. One way of demonstrating this is by entering into a *pari passu* transaction, which is carried out under identical terms (and therefore risk) as a private investor.[20] There are also rules that govern when a government can issue a state guarantee, for example to allow an undertaking to secure a loan.[21]

Now that we have a clear sense of the function of State aid rules, it is possible to focus on the UK's relationship with them and the obligations created by the EU–UK Trade and Cooperation Agreement (TCA).

---

17 Regulation (EC) 651/2014 of 17 June 2014 declaring certain categories of aid compatible with the international market in application of Articles 107 and 108 of the Treaty [2014] OJ L 187; discussed in M Morris and T Kibasi, *State Aid Rules and Brexit* (January 2019) Institute for Public Policy Research 7–8.

18 Regulation (EC) 1988/2006.

19 Commission Notice on the notion of State aid as referred to in Article 107(1) of the Treaty on the Functioning of the European Union C/2016/2946 [2016] OJ C 262 at 4.2. See also Case-305/89 *Italy v Commission ("Alfa Romeo")* [1991] ECR I-1603, paras 18 and 19.

20 Commission Notice on the notion of State aid as referred to in Article 107(1) of the Treaty on the Functioning of the European Union C/2016/2946 [2016] OJ C 262 at 86–96.

21 Commission Notice on the application of Articles 107 and 108 of the EC Treaty to State aid in the form of guarantees [2008] OJ C 155.

5.2   The UK's relationship with EU State aid rules

One common misconception about EU State aid rules is that they unfairly constrain a government's ability to implement industrial policy and nationalisation, or the taking of an undertaking into State ownership. In fact State aid rules allow a range of industrial policies, including regional development, environmental protection, and support for small businesses, so long as they do not constitute a waste of public money or distort trade.[22] Nationalisation is also perfectly permissible, so long as the government pays the market price (as demonstrated through some independent valuation) and understands that any further money granted to the entity after nationalisation would be subject to State aid rules.[23] As Crafts points out, the UK's failure to spend enough on infrastructure, reform its tax system, reform planning laws, improve innovation, and encourage research and development were more to do with political decisions taken by successive governments in Westminster than State aid rules in Brussels.[24] Figure 5.1 shows the level of expenditure on State aid within the EU in 2015, as a percentage of GDP.

Despite being a strong champion for State aid rules within the EU, successive UK governments have failed to both fully understand and take advantage of the legitimate forms of aid allowed by the rules.[25] Oxera points out that the UK spent only around €100 per capita on State aid between 2009 and 2015, as compared to €224 per capita in France and €266 in Germany over the same period.[26] Indeed, the UK's use of State aid was consistently and considerably lower than the EU average, as a percentage of GDP, throughout the period 2000–2016.[27]

Furthermore, the UK was only subject to one negative State aid ruling in the period 2000–2010 and only had a handful during the entire duration of its EU membership. By contrast, Germany had 32 during the 2000–2010

---

22 For a detailed discussion of this, see M Morris and T Kibasi, *State Aid Rules and Brexit* (January 2019) Institute for Public Policy Research.

23 ibid, 12–13.

24 N Crafts, 'Brexit and State Aid' (2017) 33(1) Oxford Review of Economic Policy 105–112, at 108–110.

25 See for example HM Government, *Review of the Balance of Competences between the United Kingdom and the European Union: Competition and Consumer Policy Report* (Summer 2014).

26 Written evidence from Oxera (CMP0012), based on data from the European Commission's *State Aid Scoreboard*, as reported in House of Lords European Union Committee, *Brexit: Competition and State Aid*, 12th Report of Session 2017–19 (2 February 2018) HL Paper 67, para 174.

27 M Morris and T Kibasi, *State Aid Rules and Brexit* (January 2019) Institute for Public Policy Research, Figure 5.2.

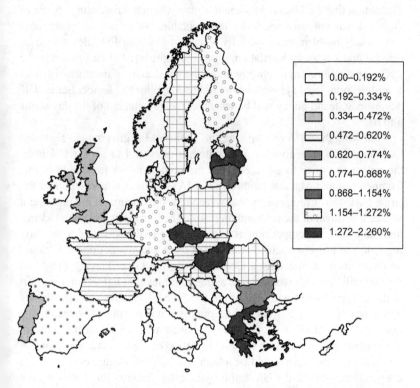

Figure 5.1 Total State aid expenditure as percent of GDP in 2015. Source: European
Commission, *State Aid Scoreboard 2016*, as printed in House of Lords
European Union Committee, *Brexit: Competition and State Aid*, 12th
Report of Session 2017–19 (2 February 2018) HL Paper 67, Chapter 6,
Figure 1. Railways are excluded from this data.

period, Italy 26, Spain 11, France 10 and the remaining Member States 43.[28]
This suggests that the UK was very compliant with EU State aid rules, having a strong approval rate under the notification procedure. In leaving the EU,
UK businesses may have lost the protection of a regime of which they were
clearly a net beneficiary. As will be discussed later, all the possible Brexit
outcomes would have significantly weakened the UK's and EU's ability to
constrain each other's use of State aid. The TCA creates far-reaching obligations, but it is no substitute for operating within the same EU State aid regime.

28 Department for Business Innovation & Skills (UK), State Aid: Frequently Asked Questions
(May 2012).

The notion that the UK could somehow stay within the regulatory sphere of State aid was not only politically unacceptable, but would have been constitutionally problematic, especially when aid violating EU rules was to be granted under primary legislation, given the supremacy of Parliament in the UK's constitution.[29] In essence, without the constraints of membership of an extra-territorial legal system like the EU as it applies to Member States, UK domestic State aid policy will be whatever the government of the day wants it to be.[30]

Following the 2016 referendum, the Theresa May government signalled its intention to 'preserve the EU State aid rules and to give a UK body the power to police those rules', and the scene was set for this to be the Competition and Markets Authority (CMA).[31] This was a key part of the 'Irish backstop' arrangements that were viewed by many on the pro-Brexit side as a betrayal of the referendum result. The European Union had identified State aid and competition as two areas key to the so-called level playing field[32] to prevent undue distortions of trade and competition.[33] It would be overseen by a Specialised Committee on the Level Playing Field and Sustainability, which would agree a maximum level of agricultural support in the UK, consistent with that of the EU. The UK's independent authority was to have the same powers as the Commission in relation to State aid. The UK would essentially have to follow EU State aid rules, ensuring 'uniform implementation, application and interpretation of the acts and provisions'.[34] To facilitate this, there would be a high level of information exchange and cooperation between the UK authority and the Commission, including the reporting of decisions. Moreover, UK courts would have to apply EU State aid law and would have the ability to submit a request to the Court of Justice

29 See F Wagner-von Papp, 'Competition Law in EU Free Trade and Cooperation Agreements (and What the UK Can Expect after Brexit)' (2017) European Yearbook of International Economic Law 301–359, at 342–343; L Wright and N Dhaun, 'State Aid in the UK Post-Brexit' (2018) 4(3) Competition Law & Policy Debate 60–66.

30 J Tomlinson and L Lovdahl Gormsen, 'Stumbling towards the UK's New Administrative Settlement: A Study of Competition Law Enforcement after Brexit' (2018) 20 Cambridge Yearbook of European Legal Studies 233–251, at 250.

31 Written evidence from the Department of Business, Energy and Industrial Strategy (CMP0041) reported in House of Lords European Union Committee, *Brexit: Competition and State Aid*, 12th Report of Session 2017–19 (2 February 2018) HL Paper 67, para 210.

32 Although some authors have suggested that 'the level playing field' amounts more to EU cherry-picking policy on its terms. See D Blake, 'Ensuring a Genuine Level Playing Field with the EU Post-Brexit' (14 March 2020), unpublished manuscript.

33 European Commission, *Draft Text of the Agreement on the New Partnership with the United Kingdom* (18 March 2020), UKTF (2020) 14, at Chapter 2, ss.1 and 2.

34 ibid, at 2.5.

of the European Union (CJEU) for a preliminary ruling, which would then be binding on UK courts.[35] The Commission would also have standing in UK courts and the right to intervene in UK cases. However, the subsequent Johnson government rejected such close alignment and the continued oversight of the CJEU, preferring instead a WTO approach to subsidies more typical in free trade agreements.

5.3 EU State aid rules vs WTO rules on subsidies

The WTO rules on subsidy control (the trade term for State aid) that the Johnson government preferred were essentially those that would have applied to the UK in the event of a no-deal Brexit. It is worth setting these out in some detail to allow us to better evaluate the subsidy control provisions of the TCA, but also to understand the regime to which the UK would be subject in the event of the TCA being abandoned. The Agreement on Subsidies and Countervailing Measures (ASCM) broadly aims to address the same kind of State assistance as defined in Article 107(1) TFEU. These are designed to prevent distortions of global trade and are divided into two categories:[36]

Prohibited subsidies – these include subsidies that require recipients to meet export targets (causing an oversupply), or a requirement to buy domestic over imported goods, thereby harming other countries' trade.

Actionable subsidies – where a country can show that the subsidy has an adverse effect on its interests. This includes harm caused to an importing country's domestic industry, harm to rival exporters from that country when competing in third markets, and where subsidies make it difficult for that firm's exporters to compete in the subsidising country's domestic market.

The agreement also gives favourable treatment to developing countries, for whom subsidies can be key to development or transition from a centrally planned economy. The lower the GNP per capita, the more favourable the

---

35 ibid, at 2.6.
36 See World Trade Organisation, 'Agreement on Subsidies and Countervailing Measures ("SCM Agreement")', www.wto.org/english/tratop_e/scm_e/subs_e.htm (accessed 13 August 2020). For a discussion, see S Switzer, 'Footloose and Fancy Free – State Aid after Brexit' (2018) 22 The Edinburgh Law Review 155–160.

treatment, but the ultimate aim is for subsidies eventually to be limited for all countries.[37] However, the WTO regime lacks teeth in a number of ways:[38]

1. The ASCM applies only to goods and not services.
2. It is based on a system of prior notification, but there is no mechanism for approving subsidies before they are implemented.
3. It relies on enforcement by States, and so individuals and businesses cannot bring action or recover damages.
4. The only remedy under WTO dispute resolution is for the measure to be withdrawn or for the injured party to take countervailing measures, not for it to be recovered with interest, and the threshold for bringing a complaint is significantly higher than under EU State aid rules.[39]

In addition, the WTO regime is arguably less sophisticated than EU State aid rules, which have both been modernised and seen a movement towards greater economic effects-based analysis.[40] This has included significantly better levels of transparency, the more effective targeting of aid, a commitment to less State aid over time and the balancing test described earlier.[41] Nonetheless, the virtues of EU State aid rules are doubted by many, who view their enforcement as too 'political', or who consider their application to have extended beyond their core purpose.[42] This is perhaps best understood by looking at how State aid law is viewed outside the EU and

---

37 World Trade Organisation, 'Agreement on Subsidies and Countervailing Measures ("SCM Agreement")', www.wto.org/english/tratop_e/scm_e/subs_e.htm (accessed 13 August 2020).
38 A Weinberger, 'State Aid Regulations after Brexit: A Good Deal for the UK?' in J Hillman and G Horlick (eds), *Legal Aspects of Brexit: Implications of the United Kingdom's Decision to Withdraw from the European Union* (Institute of International Economic Law 2017) 88–100, at 91.
39 See discussion of written evidence in House of Lords European Union Committee, *Brexit: Competition and State Aid*, 12th Report of Session 2017–19 (2 February 2018) HL Paper 67, paras 184–188.
40 See for example European Commission, Decision of 1.12.2015 on State aid for Lynemouth Power Station Biomass Conversion SA.38762 (2015/C) which the United Kingdom is planning to implement C(2015), 8441, paras 100–111, as discussed in T Chakma and N Robins, 'The Application of State Aid Rules in Various Fora: The Role of Economic Analysis' (2018) 4(3) Competition Law & Policy Debate 17–27. See also European Commission, *State Aid Action Plan, Less and Better Targeted State Aid: A Roadmap for State Aid Reform 2005 to 2009* (2005) Competition Policy Newsletter 2.
41 Haucap and Schwalbe, 'Economic Principles of State Aid Control' 17–25.
42 G Peretz and K Bacon, 'Post-Brexit Option for State Aid' (2016) unpublished manuscript.

in particular by the US media.[43] Nevertheless, it is hard to argue that the ASCM operates more effectively, especially as many WTO members either completely fail to notify or do so only very infrequently.[44] This is a major limitation, as the system relies on prior notification as the principal way of avoiding distortive subsidies.[45]

5.4 Free trade agreement provisions on State aid

Once the possibilities of membership in the European Economic Area (EEA), a customs union or partial EU oversight through 'dynamic alignment' were ruled out, a free trade agreement (FTA) became the most likely outcome of the Brexit process. Yet it was clear that the EU was keen to push for the UK to continue following EU State aid rules because of the close integration between the UK and EU economies and the volume of trade. The relevant provisions of the TCA are set out in Section 5.5, but it is first worth considering the EU's and UK's original negotiating positions and the options that were on the table.

The most obvious and common model was the Stabilisation and Association Agreements (SAAs) that the EU has entered into with neighbouring States. These are notable in how far-reaching they are in requiring the adoption of EU-based standards for the approval of aid, including the adoption of large quantities of soft law in the form of Commission guidance. They have frequently created practical problems of enforcement, where the partner country's legal system is ill-equipped to deal with EU-derived rules.[46] However, these agreements very much reflect the imbalance of negotiating power between the EU and its smaller neighbours – especially as many of the requirements of these agreements are intended to contribute to the pre-accession adoption of rules (i.e. in preparation for future EU membership) and are therefore temporary.

---

43 See for example M Bearak, 'How the EU's Ruling on Apple Explains Why Brexit Happened' (30 August 2016) *The Washington Post*; and discussion in A Weinberger, 'State Aid Regulations after Brexit: A Good Deal for the UK?' in J Hillman and G Horlick (eds), *Legal Aspects of Brexit: Implications of the United Kingdom's Decision to Withdraw from the European Union* (Institute of International Economic Law 2017) 88–100.

44 WTO, *Notification Provisions under the Agreement on Subsidies and Countervailing Measures* (G/SCM/W/546/Rec.8, 31 March 2017).

45 A Biondi, 'Brexit and State Aid Control: Four Quartets' (2018) 17(2) Competition Law Journal, 3–12, at 7.

46 M Cremona, 'State aid Control: Substance and Procedure in the European Agreements and the Stabilisation and Association Agreements' (2003) 9(3) European Law Journal 265–287.

For example, the Ukraine–EU Association Agreement, which required Ukraine to have a domestic independent regulator of State aid and to apply EU rules and guidance, is clearly not a partnership of equals. Neither is the EU–Moldova Association Agreement, which requires that any disputes relating to EU law should be referred to the CJEU for a binding judgment.[47] Ukraine and Moldova are heavily reliant on EU aid and have ambitions to become EU Member States in due course, although it was suggested that agreements like these might at least provide a useful framework for the future UK–EU relationship.[48]

Neither was it helpful to look at the model provided by Switzerland, a country not party to the EEA Agreement. Its close relationship with the EU is based on a series of bilateral agreements, of which State aid is mentioned in the 1972 Free Trade Agreement and the 1999 Agreement on Air Transport.[49] The former includes a prohibition on 'any public aid which distorts or threatens to distort competition by favouring certain undertakings or the production of certain goods'. However, this provision has limited practical application in Switzerland, and it has been suggested that it was always 'very unlikely that the EU would extend that historical accident' to the UK.[50] For example, bilateral arrangements with Switzerland are largely static, based on EU law as it was during their adoption, and contained no dynamic system of updating to ensure the agreement kept in step with changes in EU Law. The EU is now keen to address this in relation to Switzerland and also in other close bilateral relationships.[51] In 2014, the European Council signalled a strong desire to go beyond the sector-by-sector approach taken with Switzerland, because of the complexity and growing risk of legal uncertainty.[52]

---

47 Association Agreement between the European Union and the European Atomic Energy Community and their Member States, of the one part, and the Republic of Moldova, of the other part [2014] OJ L 260/4, Article 403.
48 See E Szyszczak, 'A UK Brexit Transition: To the Ukraine Model?' (November 2017) UK Trade Policy Observatory, Briefing Paper 11.
49 G Peretz, 'A Star Is Torn: Brexit and State Aid' (2016) 3 European State Aid Law Quarterly 334–337, at 335.
50 Written evidence from George Peretz, reported in House of Lords European Union Committee, *Brexit: Competition and State Aid*, 12th Report of Session 2017–19 (2 February 2018) HL Paper 67, para 181.
51 C Tobler, 'One of Many Challenges after Brexit: The Institutional Framework of an Alternative Agreement – Lessons from Switzerland and Elsewhere' (2016) 23 Maastricht Journal of European & Comparative Law 575–594, at 592.
52 Council Conclusions on a homogeneous extended single market and EU relations with Non-EU Western European Countries, 16 December 2014, para 6, cited by Tobler, 'One of Many Challenges after Brexit'.

In contrast to the EU, the UK's preference under the Johnson government was clearly to have a WTO or trade-orientated approach to subsidies. This reflected the political imperative to break from EU law, even if State aid is an area that actually benefited the UK. A notable exception is Northern Ireland, which continues to be subject to EU State aid rules in relation to some aspects of its economy, as discussed later.[53] The differing approaches were reflected in the draft negotiating texts published by each side in early 2020. It is notable that the term 'State aid' is not mentioned in the UK text – instead, it employs references to 'subsidies' signalling a clear trade dimension to its approach (Table 5.1).

It is therefore important now to consider what kind of provisions are typically contained in free trade agreements between independent jurisdictions. In a comprehensive study of free trade agreements completed in 2015, it was found that the nature and extent of the provisions that relate to competition and in particular to State aid vary hugely between individual free trade agreements.[54] The study also shows that the EU stands out as having some of the most far-reaching requirements for State aid, usually requiring close compliance with its own rules. The Comprehensive Economic and Trade Agreement (CETA) with Canada essentially sets out the sort of reporting requirements contained in the ASCM. By contrast, the EU's trade agreements with South Korea,[55] and pending agreements with Vietnam, Singapore and Japan, contain a more far-reaching prohibition on subsidies that require the parties to commit to stopping distortive effects of domestic subsidies through the application of their domestic competition law regimes.[56] Again here, the influence of the EU as the senior partner can be seen in the fact that the wording of the free trade agreements in some instances mirrors that of Article 107 and key aspects of CJEU case law.[57]

Another key sticking point was how any agreement on subsidy control would be enforced. Beyond a simple system of reporting, the mechanisms

---

53 Cabinet Office, *The UK's Approach to the Northern Ireland Protocol* (May 2020) CP226.
54 F-C Laprévote, B Can and S Frisch, 'Competition Policy within the Context of Free Trade Agreements' (September 2015) E15 Initiative Report, http://e15initiative.org/publicatio ns/competition-policy-within-the-context-of-free-trade-agreements/ (accessed 14 August 2020).
55 Free Trade Agreement between the European Union and its member States and the Republic of Korea [2011] OJ L 127/6.
56 A Biondi, 'Brexit and State Aid Control: Four Quartets' (2018) 17(2) Competition Law Journal 3–12, at 8.
57 ibid, citing the wording of the EU/Vietnam FTA referring to the compatibility of aid, and also the EU Singapore FTA, the annex of which contains a word for word repetition of the formula developed by the CJEU in Case C-280/00 *Altmark* ECL:I:EU:C:2003:415.

Table 5.1 Comparison of UK and EU draft negotiating texts 2020

UK draft text	EU draft text
Article 21.1 – Subsidy is defined according to Article 1.1 of the SCM Agreement, and is relevant only if it falls within the meaning of Article 2 of the SCM Agreement, but applies to both goods and services. Article 21.2 – Every two years each party must notify the other of details of subsidies awarded. These can either be maintained on a publicly available website or provided to the WTO under Article 25.1 of the SCM Agreement. Article 21.3 – If subsidies may adversely affect another party, they can express concerns and request consultations.	Chapter 2, Section 1. LPFS.2.1–4 – The UK must give effect to the acts and provisions set out in the Annex, but Oversight is given by a Special Committee on the Level Playing Field and Sustainability. LPFS.2.4 – The UK shall maintain an independent authority, with the necessary guarantees of independence from political or other external influence. Also decisions of the UK authority should produce 'the same legal effects as those which comparable decisions of the European Commission acting under the acts and provisions listed in ANNEX LPFS-X produce within the EU or its Member States'. LPFS.2.5 – The two authorities will cooperate and consult each other on all draft decisions they intend to adopt in respect of measures that affect trade between them. LPFS.2.6 – UK courts can request the CJEU to give a preliminary ruling on a question and that will be binding on the referring courts or tribunals of the United Kingdom. The Commission shall have legal standing before courts or tribunals of the UK. LPFD.2.77 – Parties may request detailed information where they feel aid granted by the other party may lead to a serious risk of undue distortion to trade or competition.

Sources: HM Government, DRAFT UK-EU Comprehensive Free Trade Agreement (CFTA), 27 February 2020, www.gov.uk/government/publications/our-approach-to-the-future-rel ationship-with-the-eu (accessed 15 August 2020). European Commission, Draft Text of the Agreement on the New Partnership with the United Kingdom, 18 March 2020, UKTF (2020) 14, https://ec.europa.eu/info/sites/info/files/200318-draft-agreement-gen.pdf (accessed 15 August 2020).

available included binding arbitration,[58] or the creation of a special court or tribunal, such as the European Free Trade Area (EFTA) Court. However, the EFTA Court applies Article 61 of the EEA Agreement (the relevant provision on State aid) in precisely the same way as Article 107 TFEU and so

---

58 See J Bryant and C Drews, 'The Brexit's Repercussions on International Arbitration' (2019) 6 Yearbook on International Arbitration 63.

is de facto bound to the jurisprudence of the CJEU.[59] Similarly, the EFTA Surveillance Authority essentially undertakes the role of the Commission in enforcing State aid rules. Another common approach is a joint committee, made up of equal representation from the two parties and supported by technical groups. This might be described as primarily a political or diplomatic method of dispute resolution. It exists under the EEA Agreement and the North American Free Trade Agreement (NAFTA), for example.[60] By contrast, CETA[61] and the EU–Vietnam FTA contain provisions for disputes to be resolved by binding arbitration panels. These can operate through the WTO's dispute settlement system through requests to the WTO Dispute Settlement Body, although this process is time-consuming. Crucially, while the outcome of arbitration is binding, it does not have automatic effect domestically and governments can delay or ignore its full implementation. Neither is it backed by the ability to impose fines for non-compliance, in the way that the CJEU can directly sanction Member States. The consequences consist instead of mitigating measures, or the suspension of all or part of the trade agreement. An additional obstacle came from the EU's traditional hostility to the use of arbitration in bilateral agreements on the basis that it undermines the 'autonomy' of EU law in areas such as State aid, which are considered to be of exclusive EU competence.[62] Accordingly, the EU's strong preference was for the UK to continue being bound to EU State aid rules under domestic law, with some CJEU oversight.

5.5 Subsidy control in the UK–EU Trade and Cooperation Agreement

The TCA constituted a significant compromise on State aid by both sides. The UK is not directly subject to EU State aid rules and has escaped any oversight by the CJEU (except as it relates to the Northern Ireland Protocol). In addition, the agreement employs WTO language – *subsidy control*, with not a single mention of State aid, despite that being the phrase used in the

59 M Segura, E Olafsson and M Clayton, 'Brexit, the EEA and the EU State Aid Rules' (2019) 1 European State Aid Law Quarterly 3–14, at 7; G Peretz, 'A Star Is Torn: Brexit and State Aid' (2016) 3 European State Aid Law Quarterly 334–337.

60 G Peretz (n 59), paras 31–34.

61 Comprehensive Economic and Trade Agreement (CETA) between Canada and the European Union and its Member States (30 October 2016) [2017] OJ L 11/23.

62 A Biondi, 'Brexit and State Aid Control: Four Quartets' (2018) 17(2) Competition Law Journal, 3–12, at 10, cites Opinion 2/15 *Free Trade Agreement between the European Union and the Republic of Singapore*, ECLI:EU:C:2017:376 and Case C-284/16 *Slovak Republic v. Achmea BV*, ECLI:EU:C:2018:158.

Withdrawal Agreement. Yet the substance of the provisions set out in Title XI, Chapter 3 are closely related to EU State aid rules and their practical application. Furthermore, unlike the chapter on competition law, the subsidy control provisions are underpinned by powers to impose retaliatory measures and a system of binding arbitration.

5.5.1 The subsidy control provisions of the TCA

A subsidy is defined in the TCA as financial assistance that 'confers an economic advantage on one or more economic actors' that 'benefits ... certain economic actors over others in relation to the production of certain goods or services' and 'has, or could have, an effect on trade or investment between' the EU and UK.[63] Article 3.4 is of particular importance as it sets out the principles that underpin an effective subsidy control system that each side is obliged to maintain.

In Table 5.2 it can be seen how the principles that underpin the system of subsidy control to be adopted by the UK under the TCA are essentially an expression of the balancing test undertaken by the Commission in determining whether aid is lawful.

The similarities do not end there. The references made in Article 107 to the exclusion of subsidies granted to compensate 'damage caused by natural disasters' and 'subsidies of a social character' are contained in Article 3.2. Article 3.3 – services of public economic interest, when taken together with the principles of Article 3.4, largely reflects the criteria set out in *Altmark* for determining whether aid granted in relation to 'services of general economic interest' are compatible with Article 107.[64] This refers to economic activities that public authorities identify as being of particular importance to their citizens (such as public transport or postal services) and which would not be supplied (or would be supplied under different conditions) if there were no public intervention.

5.5.2 Applying the principles and dealing with disputes

The competent courts and tribunals must review subsidy decisions taken by the granting authority and impose remedies, including suspension, prohibition, the award of damages and recovery of the subsidy.[65] They must also hear claims from 'interested parties', meaning 'any natural or legal

---

63 TCA, Article 3.1(1).
64 Case C-280/00 *Altmark* ECL:I:EU:C:2003:415.
65 TCA, Article 3.10.

Table 5.2 Comparison of the UK–EU TCA subsidy control principles and the balancing test in EU State aid

TCA, Title XI, Article 3.4: Principles	*The balancing test in EU State aid*[a]
a) subsidies pursue a specific public policy objective to remedy an identified market failure or to address an equity rationale such as social difficulties or distributional concerns ('the objective');	1. Is the aid measure aimed at a well-defined objective of common interest?
b) subsidies are proportionate and limited to what is necessary to achieve the objective;	2. Is the aid well designed to deliver the objective of common interest, i.e. does the proposed aid address the market failure or other objectives?
c) subsidies are designed to bring about a change of economic behaviour of the beneficiary that is conducive to achieving the objective and that would not be achieved in the absence of subsidies being provided;	I. Is the aid an appropriate policy instrument to address the policy objective concerned?
d) subsidies should not normally compensate for the costs the beneficiary would have funded in the absence of any subsidy;	II. Is there an incentive effect, i.e. does the aid change the behaviour of the aid recipient?
e) subsidies are an appropriate policy instrument to achieve a public policy objective and that objective cannot be achieved through other less distortive means;	III. Is the aid measure proportionate to the problem tackled, i.e. could the same change in behaviour not be obtained with less aid?
f) subsidies' positive contributions to achieving the objective outweigh any negative effects, in particular the negative effects on trade or investment between the Parties.	3. Are the distortions of competition and effect on trade limited, so that the overall balance is positive?

[a] From European Commission, Common Principles for an Economic Assessment of the Compatibility of State Aid, under Article 87.3 at 9.

person, economic actor or association of economic actors whose interest might be affected by the granting of a subsidy, in particular the beneficiary, economic actors competing with the beneficiary or relevant trade associations'.[66] Where an interested party has successfully challenged a decision to grant a subsidy (e.g. because the grantor failed to apply the principles correctly), there must be an effective mechanism in place for ordering the

---

66 TCA, Article 3.7(6).

recovery of the aid. However, Acts of Parliament are beyond the scope of these obligations.

Although there is a requirement that the UK maintain an independent authority with 'an appropriate role' in its subsidy control regime, there is no requirement that it create an ex ante system of notification and clearance.[67] Instead, details of subsidies must be published within six months and the EU and UK can request information from each other about a subsidy that raises concerns.[68] Where there are more serious concerns about the subsidy causing a negative effect on trade or investment between the UK and EU, the parties can enter consultations following the supply of information. If a resolution is not reached within 60 days from the date of delivery of the request for information, the requesting party 'may unilaterally take appropriate measures if there is evidence that a subsidy' will cause a significant negative effect to trade.[69] These must be notified in advance and an attempt made to find a solution. Their finding that it will cause a significant negative effect must be based on fact and not allegation and the measures taken must be strictly necessary and proportionate. While they are in place, an arbitration panel will be convened to resolve the dispute. The panel will make a decision as to whether the remedial measure is consistent, whether either party participated fully in consultations and whether the necessary reporting and notification requirements were undertaken. Neither party can invoke the WTO agreement in relation to the measures. Finally, the arbitration panel will not generally have jurisdiction to interfere with the interpretation of the subsidy control provisions by the independent authority or with the finding of a court or tribunal.[70]

Therefore, unlike the TCA chapter on competition law, the subsidy control provisions are detailed and underpinned by a system of unilateral retaliatory measures pending the outcome of binding arbitration. This was a sensible outcome, as it essentially provides the EU with protection of the 'level playing field' by binding the UK to the core principles of State aid and requiring them to adopt many of its practical aspects (e.g. an independent authority, review by the courts, remedial powers including the recovery of incompatible aid, and the ability for interested parties to bring claims). As outlined, the mechanism for enforcing the subsidy control provisions go

67 TCA, Article 3.9.
68 TCA, Article 3.7.
69 TCA, Article 3.12(3).
70 TCA, Article 3.13.

beyond WTO rules and what is typical in free trade agreements.[71] In return, the UK enjoys tariff-free trade on goods, but is outside the scope of EU law and any oversight by the CJEU (except in relation to Northern Ireland, as discussed in Section 5.5.3). As a dualist legal system, any international treaty the UK adopts is only given effect domestically through an act of Parliament.[72] The UK is bound to the agreement as a matter of international law and is subject to the enforcement mechanisms contained therein.

It is important to point out that these mechanisms will benefit the UK – especially given that it has historically been a net beneficiary of EU State aid rules. However, they will be inferior to the protections afforded when the UK was a Member State. This is because UK and EU firms will only be able to bring claims before the courts and tribunals where they have standing to do so. If they are affected by a subsidy in the other jurisdiction but have no standing there, the only recourse will be to make a complaint to the UK government or to the Commission to dispute the subsidy on their behalf. The UK or the EU can either do this through the formal remedial processes set out in the TCA or by exercising the 'right to intervene with the permission' in court or tribunal proceedings in each other's jurisdiction.[73]

5.5.3 *Goods, services and Northern Ireland*

One peculiar aspect of the subsidy control provisions is that they govern the trade of goods *and services*. This goes significantly beyond WTO rules on subsidies (which generally concern only goods) and the nature of the TCA itself, which does very little to facilitate frictionless trade in services. For example, there is nothing to maintain the mutual recognition of professional qualifications and accreditation. It is also notable that the Northern Ireland protocol requires that EU State aid rules apply to trade between Northern Ireland and the EU, but the protocol only covers goods (to avoid the need for a hard border on the island of Ireland) and not services.[74] In practice, the application of EU State aid law on goods traded between Northern Ireland

---

71 DD Sokol, 'Order without (Enforceable) Law: Why Countries Enter into Non-Enforceable Competition Policy Chapters in Free Trade Agreements' (2008) 83 Chicago-Kent Law Review 231.

72 See discussion in HM Government, *Enforcement and Dispute Resolution: A Future Partnership Paper* (23 August 2017); O Solano and A Sennekamp, 'Competition Provisions in Regional Trade Agreements' (2006) OECD Trade Policy Paper No. 31, paras 21–22.

73 TCA, Article 3.10(2).

74 It also applies to the Northern Ireland electricity market. See Revised Protocol to the Withdrawal Agreement (New Protocol on Ireland / Northern Ireland) (17 October 2019), Article 10.

and the EU was likely to have a wider scope than intended anyway. For example, most aid granted in Great Britain might be said to have some effect on trade between Northern Ireland and the EU, if the recipients have a UK-wide presence. Although the protocol only covers goods and the electricity market, it is also likely that subsidies provided to the service sector could be deemed to have an effect on trade in goods, for example aid to transport or banking providers.[75] Having provisions in the TCA that closely map onto EU State aid rules and which cover both goods and services may help to alleviate the danger of the European Commission reviewing aid primarily targeting Great Britain. It may also facilitate greater future cooperation and bilateral agreements on services.[76]

5.6   The role of the independent authority

It is worth exploring the role of the 'operationally independent authority' that the UK is required to maintain as a counterpart to the European Commission for the purposes of having an 'appropriate role' in its subsidy control regime.[77] The question of whether the UK should adopt a domestic system of subsidy control, and who should administer it, was entirely unresolved when the TCA was agreed upon. Some within the Johnson government called for there to be no independent regulator and for subsidy control to instead be subject to a light-touch regime.[78] This may have been motivated by a misunderstanding of the State aid rules, or part of a negotiating strategy, or may have represented a genuine intention to move industrial policy into a new era of significant state assistance. There may also have been a desire to adopt an aggressive business taxation strategy in order to undercut the

---

75 See European Commission, *Notice to Stakeholders: Withdrawal of the United Kingdom and EU Rules in the Field of State Aid* (18 January 2021).

76 See 'Brexit: Sunak Suggests EU Access for Financial Services Will Exceed Deal' *The Guardian* (28 December 2020) and I Jozepa, M Ward and D Harari, *Trade in Services and Brexit* (December 2019) House of Commons Briefing Paper 8586.

77 TCA, Article 3.9(1).

78 'Cummings Leads Push for Light-Touch UK State-Aid Regime after Brexit' *Financial Times* (28 July 2020). See also Department for Business, Energy & Industrial Strategy, *UK Internal Market* (July 2020) CP278, paras 55–56. See also comments by a former Cabinet Member under the May Government: D Gauke, 'Without a Proper State Aid Regime, the UK is Unlikely to Reach a Deal with Brussels' Conservative Home (1 August 2020). For a discussion of some of the potential benefits of no State aid restrictions within the UK, see generally A Weinberger, 'State Aid Regulations after Brexit: A Good Deal for the UK?' in J Hillman and G Horlick (eds), *Legal Aspects of Brexit: Implications of the United Kingdom's Decision to Withdraw from the European Union* (Institute of International Economic Law 2017) 88–100.

EU and attract foreign investment.[79] Indeed, even the Future Relationship document published under the May government suggested that the future relationship 'would not fetter ... [the UK's] sovereign discretion on tax'.[80] This inferred that taxes would lie outside any agreement on State aid, when in fact the TCA contains provisions preventing unfair tax competition (Title XI, Chapter 5) and the subsidy control provisions require transparency for subsidies that come in the form of tax measures (Article 3.7(2)).[81] Their inclusion reflects how the European Commission has become increasingly aggressive in its targeting of tax measures, which it argues are distorting trade and allowing big companies to evade taxes through sweetheart deals with individual governments on special terms.[82] Indeed, immediately following the end of the transition period, the European Parliament voted to add UK overseas territories including Guernsey and Jersey to an EU tax havens blacklist.[83]

5.6.1 Why have an independent authority?

Superficially, one might be compelled by the idea that an elected government should have the freedom to spend taxpayers' money as it sees fit. Yet there are two good reasons why a government might submit to an independent regulator and the courts, even if this constrains their ability to conduct industrial policy. The first is that a mutual submitting to controls on government behaviour (whether through EU State aid rules or a free trade agreement chapter on subsidies) is the price that has to be paid for limiting the ability of other countries to gain an international advantage over their own domestic firms. In particular, without it there is a greater risk that subsidies cancel each other out or that governments get drawn into a mutually ruinous subsidy war. These unwanted effects can occur domestically as well as internationally, due to the UK's complex system of devolution that

---

79 S Hirsbrunner, 'How to Please Your Sweethearts When You Are Divorcing: The UK Government's Ability to Offer Incentives to Foreign Investors after Brexit' (2016) 4 European State Aid Quarterly 504–507.

80 HM Government, *The Future Relationship between the UK and the EU* (July 2018) para 110.

81 On the interaction between State aid and corporate tax avoidance, see S Marco Colino, 'The Long Arm of State Aid Law: Crushing Corporate Tax Avoidance' (2020) 44(2) Fordham International Law Journal 397.

82 The Commission ordered the Netherlands to recover €25.7 million in tax advantages from Starbucks in 2015, Ireland to recover €14.3 billion in tax benefits from Apple in 2016; and Luxembourg to recover €282.7 million in tax benefits from Amazon in 2017.

83 See 'MEPs vote to Add Channel and British Virgin Islands to Tax Haven Blacklist' *The Guardian* (22 January 2021).

gives spending powers to the devolved governments of Scotland, Wales and Northern Ireland, as well as mayors and other local administrations. Having a clear set of State aid rules and an independent regulatory regime will help avoid regional subsidy wars and the danger of deepening regional divides by virtue of 'successful' regions having deeper pockets with which to attract further investment.[84] Both the Scottish and Welsh governments were opposed to the UK government having control of State aid and supported the establishment of an independent State aid regulator, but only with their involvement.[85] This was in part to avoid exclusive control by the Westminster government, but also to avoid the regime bending in the direction of the UK government of the day.

The second is to do with *self-control*. An independent State aid regime makes it easier for governments to rebuff the huge lobbying efforts and political pressure that can result in 'irrational' subsidies being conceded, especially if that pressure comes from a marginal constituency, from a devolved administration or in the run-up to a general election.[86] It can then be advantageous for a government to tie its hands credibly so that it cannot grant subsidies for short-term political gain. Furthermore, it greatly reduces wasteful lobbying pressure if everyone knows that there are clear limits as to what aid can be offered.[87] The UK has an appalling history of failing to successfully 'pick winners' through industrial policies of the 1960s and 1970s. Rather than being targeted where they would have the most effect, large sums of taxpayers' money were wasted propping up

---

84 This point is also made in the Brexit Competition Law Working Group, *Conclusions and Recommendations* (July 2017) para 4.2, where it states 'it would be appropriate for the UK to create an "internal" discipline on subsidy policy'.

85 Written evidence from the Scottish Government (CMP0039) and Welsh Government (CMP0043), reported in House of Lords European Union Committee, *Brexit: Competition and State Aid*, 12th Report of Session 2017–19 (2 February 2018) HL Paper 67, para 190–192.

86 There may also be other political reasons why inefficient State aid is granted. For example, the lobbying incentive is greater for inefficient firms, so it is not that government policy picks losers, but the 'losers' who pick government policy. See Richard E Baldwin and Frédéric Robert-Nicoud, 'Entry and Asymmetric Lobbying: Why Governments Pick Losers' (2007) 5(5) Journal of the European Economic Association 1064. Also, politicians may want to signal their commitment to constituents despite the cost; see Mathias Dewatripont and Paul Seabright '"Wasteful" Public Spending and State Aid Control' (2006) 4(2–3) Journal of the European Economic Association 513.

87 Similar concerns used to be raised in connection to monetary policy before governments across the world realised that a more stable economy could be achieved by putting monetary policy in the hands of an independent central bank. Independent decision-making by competition agencies such as the CMA provide another important example of designing institutions positively to limit short-term political discretion.

failing or inefficient production in a relatively small number of industries, such as car production.[88] The way in which governments can make spending decisions primarily in a reactive manner is demonstrated by the May government's comfort letter to Nissan in October 2016, apparently aimed at compensating the company for any Brexit costs to its Sunderland car plant, but probably on a collision course with EU State aid rules.[89] A freedom of information request by a BBC journalist indicated that Nissan had written to the government highlighting that it was 'the global leader in electric cars' and noting a number of policies that would make the UK more attractive for a major investment in electric cars.[90] Several of these suggestions were announced as government initiatives in the following weeks. These may or may not be good initiatives, but the point is that sector deals are likely to be tweaked towards the advantage of individual large firms with a strong negotiating hand.

The preceding arguments also tend to point towards the need for an independent State aid regulator. In March 2018 the May government announced that 'the UK should be prepared to establish a full, UK-wide subsidy control framework' and that this would be operated by the CMA as 'an independent UK State aid authority'.[91] This was repeated in a 2019 briefing paper on the withdrawal agreement.[92] In March 2019, the CMA even published a draft guidance on State aid notifications and reporting in light of the withdrawal agreement and a draft statutory instrument was prepared.[93] By summer 2020, the CMA's role as the UK's independent State aid regulator was in some doubt, much to the confusion of the House of Lords EU Internal Market Sub-Committee, which could not get the government to clarify its

---

88 See generally C Wren, *Industrial Subsidies: The UK Experience* (Macmillan 1996).

89 See for example 'Nissan Was Offered Secret State Aid to Cope with Brexit, Minister Concedes' *The Guardian* (4 February 2019).

90 Chris Cook, 'What did ministers discuss with Nissan? *BBC News* (24 March 2017) www.bbc.co.uk/news/uk-39387439 (accessed 28 April 2017).

91 Letter from Andrew Griffiths, Minister for Small Business, Consumers and Corporate Responsibility, to Lord Whitty, Chair of House of Lords EU Internal Market Sub-Committee, 28 March 2018. Discussed in 'A View from the CMA: Brexit and Beyond' speech by Michael Grenfell, CMA Executive Director – Enforcement, 16 May 2018.

92 House of Commons Briefing Paper, *The UK's EU Withdrawal Agreement*, No 08453, 11 April 2019, p. 44.

93 Competition and Markets Authority, *Draft Procedural Guidance on State Aid Notifications and Reporting* (4 March 2019) CMA104; Draft Statutory Instrument, 2019 Exiting the European Union, Competition, The State Aid (EU Exit) Regulations 2019, under para 1(1) of schedule 7 to the European Union (Withdrawal) Act 2018.

position.[94] Nonetheless, the requirement that the UK set up an independent authority was set out in the negotiating document published by the EU in March 2020.[95]

5.6.2 *The UK subsidy control regime*

While the exact design of the UK's new subsidy control regime was not known at the time of writing, it was clear that it was heading for a far more flexible approach than that of the EU State aid regime. In particular, there were no plans to replicate its ex ante approval and block exemption system, and the role of the independent authority was potentially far weaker than that of the European Commission. In its 2021 consultation on the new proposed regime, the government was quick to dismiss any suggestion of a return to the wasteful subsidisation policies of the past.[96] The focus of the new regime was instead on priorities, including the 'levelling up' of poorer regions of the UK, achieving the net zero carbon target and dealing with market failure.[97] Devolved administrations and local authorities were to enjoy greater flexibility in making spending decisions, in the absence of any ex ante approval mechanism, but subsidies would not be allowed to distort competition by giving businesses in one nation or region an unfair competitive advantage over those elsewhere in the UK.[98] Much was centred on what public authorities must demonstrate to show they have not fallen foul of the subsidy control principles. The identity and powers of the new independent body responsible for overseeing the regime was also unknown at the time of writing. A key question was the extent to which it would have direct enforcement powers, or have to rely on court proceedings.[99]

The CMA is the natural choice in terms of expertise and its close working relationship with the European Commission, but undertaking the role would be challenging nonetheless. It may be that the CMA was not keen to take on responsibility for a role that could frequently put it on a collision course

---

94 See letter of 3 April 2020 from Baroness Donaghy, Chair of the EU Internal Market Sub-Committee, to Paul Scully MP, Minister for Small Business, Consumers and Labour Markets.

95 European Commission, *Draft Text of the Agreement on the New Partnership with the United Kingdom* (18 March 2020), UKTF (2020) 14, at 2.4.

96 Department for Business, Energy & Industrial Strategy, *Subsidy Control: Designing a New Approach for the UK* (February 2021). See in particular the Foreword by the Secretary of State.

97 ibid, at 1 and 28.

98 ibid, at 36.

99 ibid, at 118.

with the decisions of public bodies and government departments.[100] It may have been exposed to political sensitivities involving spending decisions by the devolved administrations. There was also the problem that State aid is different to other areas of competition and so existing CMA expertise and experience would not necessarily lend itself to effective review of subsidy decisions. Second, subsidy control would constitute yet another significant increase in its workload, with the need for an appropriate increase in staffing and resources, to reflect the nature of its new role. This would come in addition to the increased mergers and antitrust caseload.

There may be scope for the UK to establish a subsidy control regime that is more efficient than the current EU notification procedure. This was identified in evidence submitted to the House of Lords Committee looking into Brexit, competition and State aid in 2017. The UK State Aid Law Association noted that even relatively straightforward cases of subsidies could take six months or more to complete and that this was compounded when it was being awarded by local government, as it could take time simply to get central government to make the request.[101] It was supported by evidence from the Local Government Association, which said it found the EU State aid regime complex and that the cost and time needed to clear aid was often thought to be prohibitive.[102] Accordingly, a clear priority was to simplify the rules for smaller regional aid packages.

5.7 Concluding remarks

The TCA has struck a fair balance between the negotiating positions of the UK and the EU. It delivers on the UK breaking free of the oversight of EU institutions and courts, except as they relate to the Northern Ireland Protocol, while also creating binding principles that help ensure a level playing field. The language used in the TCA has been sanitised to some extent of EU State aid terminology. Nonetheless, we have observed how the principles and remedies required are essentially an expression of the EU State aid regime, which is compliant with the requirements of the TCA from the outset. We

---

100 Written evidence from the British Institute of International and Comparative Law (CMP0010) reported in House of Lords European Union Committee, *Brexit: Competition and State Aid*, 12th Report of Session 2017–19 (2 February 2018) HL Paper 67, para 200.

101 Written evidence from the UK State Aid Bar Association (CMP0038), reported in House of Lords European Union Committee, *Brexit: Competition and State Aid*, 12th Report of Session 2017–19 (2 February 2018) HL Paper 67, para 37.

102 Written evidence from the Local Government Association (CMP0021), reported in House of Lords European Union Committee, *Brexit: Competition and State Aid*, 12th Report of Session 2017–19 (2 February 2018) HL Paper 67, para 38.

have also demonstrated how the Johnson government's scepticism about subsidy control was largely unfounded. There are significant benefits to the UK from the obligations created by the TCA, and any ambitions of using selective subsidies to give the UK a competitive advantage would likely have been inefficient and hampered its efforts to reach free trade agreements by putting the UK in conflict with WTO rules. Reliance on a combination of the independent authority and the courts should help to deflect pressure from individual industries and businesses that risk skewing how government spending is used and from distorting competition in UK markets. It is important that interested parties have the right to challenge aid and that the TCA provides a way for the UK to challenge EU aid that adversely affects trade with the UK, albeit using mechanisms that are inferior to what existed when the UK was an EU Member State.

Conclusion

Brexit has happened. The UK has withdrawn from the European Union and a trade and cooperation agreement is in place to govern trade between the two jurisdictions, including in relation to competition law and State aid. The implications for competition law enforcement were not widely debated in political circles, but there was clearly considerable thought by the Competition and Markets Authority (CMA), the Department for Business, and by competition law academics and practitioners from the time of the fateful vote to the end of the transition period and agreement at the end of 2020. This book has sought to give a fairly comprehensive account of the key issues, consequences and developments, and in this brief concluding chapter we shall try to give a review and overview of the salient points and areas for potential future research and review.

The first set of issues concerns the legal apparatus, institutions and cooperation mechanisms, particularly in relation to antitrust rules. The first is to note that the EU Commission, in conjunction with the other Member State national competition authorities (NCAs) as part of the European Competition Network (ECN) and in line with Regulation 1/2003 and the 2004 Network Notice, will continue to apply the rules in Articles 101 and 102 of the Treaty on the Functioning of the European Union (TFEU) to infringements which produce anti-competitive effects in the EU. Accordingly, UK-based businesses which operate in EU markets will need to continue to consider compliance with those EU prohibitions in order to avoid fines and other sanctions/remedies being imposed. Being outside the EU legal framework does not shield businesses from the EU law rules operating in the single market. In relation to domestic UK competition law there will also be no necessary change. The system of market investigations will remain untouched and unaffected by Brexit.

The primary UK antitrust rules, the Chapters I and II prohibitions of the Competition Act 1998, are directly modelled on the EU prohibitions in Articles 101 and 102. Their introduction was a purely domestic choice, not forced harmonisation. Accordingly, in the short term at least, and subject to the revised interpretative requirements in s.60A of the Competition Act, there is no clamour to make any modifications to these central rules nor the institutions which enforce them – primarily the CMA (and sectoral regulators) and the Competition Appeal Tribunal (CAT). However, the matter is slightly complicated by the retained law nature of some provisions of EU law, notably certain Block Exemption Regulations and the regulations implementing the Antitrust Damages Directive. Enforcement of the rules is certainly an area of potential uncertainty and change, given in particular the overlapping competencies of the EU and UK competition institutions that may in the future be looking at the same anti-competitive behaviour in terms of its respective impacts and effects on the EU and UK markets. A key point here is to note that the CMA has undertaken considerable preparation for the new era and ensured in its advocacy role that it would be greater resourced for future post-Brexit challenges. How will the CMA develop its enforcement and prioritisation strategies in light of Brexit? Research by Rodger has demonstrated that in fact the UK authorities have investigated very few infringements of EU competition law and have tended to focus on mainly localised infringements of the domestic rules. It will be interesting to observe to what extent this changes and the CMA will have an appetite to consider also bigger cases, such as (for example) Google's alleged anti-competitive behaviour, alongside the EU's investigation processes. This leads to the final point regarding cooperation in enforcement. The UK will no longer be part of the ECN and its system of cooperation and shared confidential information, and it is hoped that the CMA will be able to build and maintain effective cooperation mechanisms with the Commission/ECN and also with other State competition authorities worldwide.

The second set of issues, canvassed in Chapter 2, concerns the future development of the central prohibitions in the Competition Act 1998, modelled on Articles 101 and 102, and the extent to which there may be scope for future divergence in the interpretation and application of the two sets of rules. Chapter 2 discussed at length the new revised interpretative requirements in s.60A of the Competition Act 1998. Gone is the absolute requirement for consistency of approach in relation to the substance of Articles 101 and 102 and with rulings by the CJEU in particular, but we need to closely observe the extent to which the enforcement authorities and courts react to the new flexibility derived from s.60A. It is unlikely that there will be any changes in relation to horizontal agreements and in particular any of the legal issues relating to hard-core cartels, but will we see any clear blue water in relation to the treatment of vertical agreements? Our view is that this is very unlikely, especially in the short to medium term. The UK authorities have not in any event applied Article 101 to market integration issues.

Indeed, consistent with the VABER prohibition of resale price maintenance (RPM), the CMA (and its predecessor the Office of Fair Trading [OFT]) have sanctioned numerous instances of vertical and hub-and-spoke resale price maintenance arrangements over the years. This is clearly seen as a pro-consumer enforcement strategy and is likely to remain a key priority in the coming years. More policy-driven enforcement issues, such as the scope of the exceptions to the Chapter I prohibition and the application of existing and future revised versions of the Block Exemption Regulations, may potentially be areas for review and a differentiated UK-specific approach in the future. Nonetheless, it is clear that the area with the greatest likelihood for potential divergence from existing and future EU law approaches is in relation to the application of the abuse of dominance prohibition, notwithstanding the identical terminology of the domestic and EU rules in Chapter II and Article 102, respectively (apart from the effect on inter-state trade requirement obviously). As indicated in Chapter 2, this would simply reflect the fact that there has been greater controversy and disagreement historically and globally about the appropriate content and scope of competition law rules in relation to unilateral conduct. They lie more closely on the fault line between free markets and State intervention in markets which may interfere with 'business' liberty and contract and intellectual property rights. Different legal systems, based partly on political, economic and social beliefs, approach these issues and the role of fairness in the context of unilateral conduct rules in different ways. This general setting suggests that the UK competition authorities and courts, despite the relatively limited abuse enforcement experience to date, may both prioritise enforcement and interpret the law on abuse in a different way from the Commission at the EU level. Moreover, there is particular scope for diverging approaches to be adopted in relation to a wide range of abuse-related issues in digital markets, currently a key focal point of competition authorities. Of course, both the CMA and the Commission will continue to participate in the International Competition Network, and this form of informal communication may at least diminish the scope for any wide divergence in legal approaches.

Private enforcement of competition rules, whether by business or consumers claiming to have suffered losses as a result of an alleged competition law infringement, has historically played a predominant role in the antitrust enforcement landscape in the US. Competition litigation has increased in significance across the EU and in the UK in particular in recent years, and Chapter 3 assessed various issues in order to allow us to reflect on the potential impact of Brexit. In the EU, the UK courts and the CAT in particular have developed expertise and have been perceived as a leader in the enforcement of EU competition law rights by private parties. There are many rules and mechanisms to facilitate that litigation – some driven by EU law itself, including the role of the CJEU in ensuring the effectiveness of EU law rights (e.g. in *Crehan*) and the introduction of the Antitrust Damages Directive. Nonetheless, the reality is that many of the rules, institutions and levers to enhance the availability of damages and other remedies, have been common law or statutory developments in the UK (and the UK's internal legal systems), such as the rules on discovery, the introduction and increasing role/knowledge of the specialist CAT, and the expertise of the private Bar. Two issues driven purely at the domestic level have been key: litigation funding developments and the Consumer Rights Act 2015 collective redress scheme, as considered recently in *Merricks v Mastercard*. Future research should focus on the extent to which those various mechanisms and developing experience will be sufficient to overcome the perceived limitations consequent to Brexit in this area, notably the position of EU law as foreign law and Commission decisions no longer providing binding effect for claimants; and the impact of withdrawal from the Brussels 1a Regime on jurisdiction for international competition law claims, in particular whether parties will be more reluctant to sue here in the absence of clear expedited recognition and enforcement rules. We should also observe whether our adoption of certain Antitrust Damages Directive provisions may be reconsidered, for instance by rowing back on the more pro-claimant set of rules on limitation introduced thereunder. There is optimism here that the CAT (and High Court) will remain a central forum for European antitrust litigation, but other legal systems such as the Netherlands are seeking to compete, and the EU-wide dispersal of the trucks cartel litigation has enhanced experience of competition litigation in a range of EU national courts.

Merger control is a particularly significant aspect of any competition law system in practice, and Chapter 4 considered the ramifications of the UK withdrawal from the EU on merger control practice and the future of UK merger control. The fundamental change following Brexit is a shift from a one-stop-shop system of control to the existence of two parallel regimes at the UK and EU level. Of course, UK and EU merger controls have co-existed for a number of years, but the one-stop shop under the EU Merger Regulation 139/2004 ensured that any particular merger could be assessed under the EU Merger Regulation by the Commission or by the CMA under the Enterprise Act 2002 but excluded assessment by both. The motivations were to make merger clearance easier by limiting the regulatory burdens and thereby facilitate beneficial mergers. Indeed very few qualifying mergers under either system are actually blocked. Post-Brexit, advisers will have to assess if any proposed merger qualifies under the different thresholds of either or both UK and EU merger control. This will inevitably in some cases make the regulatory clearance process more complicated: mergers which qualify for assessment under both systems may have to be notified (note voluntary UK context) and assessed, involving two different sets of paper-work, two regulatory authorities, two slightly varying regulatory schedules and time limits, two similar but different substantive tests, two sets of remedy proposals, etc. The UK and EU merger control systems are broadly the same, but any proposed merger involving a double regulatory hurdle will inevitably involve more time, money and bureaucracy, and is less likely to proceed. As noted, the CMA's non-discretionary workload in relation to merger control will inevitably increase, and researchers should seek to observe the impact of this on the future balance of the CMA's workload as between merger control and its antitrust enforcement work. Moreover, it will be particularly interesting should the CMA and Commission adopt conflicting positions in relation to any particular merger simultaneously assessed under both sets of rules. It may be that the rules will diverge in particular in relation to the approach to mergers in digital markets generally and to killer acquisitions in particular, an area of considerable contemporary regulatory focus. Moreover, there is a concern that UK merger control in the coming years may become more protectionist, and that the scope of the exceptional public interest rules continues to expand. Finally, Brexit may require reconsideration of the voluntary notification nature of the system, and both the UK and EU authorities should also reflect on the respective thresholds for mergers to qualify for review under each system.

The final set of issues considered in Chapter 5 relate to State aid, or subsidy control as it has come to be known in the EU–UK Trade and Cooperation Agreement (TCA). We saw how the use of selective subsidies can be hugely distortive to competition and international trade, and constitute a very significant waste of public money. Whatever the UK government's ambitions concerning subsidies, there were always going to be constraints on the UK's ability to use taxpayer money, by virtue of the World Trade Organization (WTO) subsidy control rules. The question was simply the extent and range of those constraints in relation to future trade with the EU. From the moment that the UK government chose to interpret the 2016 referendum vote as a decision to completely leave the jurisdiction of the Court of Justice of the European Union (CJEU), the prospect of continued application of EU State aid became politically unacceptable. The TCA provided a very sensible and diplomatic solution to the standoff that saw negotiations of the agreement go right to the wire. The provisions are not State aid – they are 'subsidy control' thereby using the more palatable language of trade agreements. Yet the principles agreed largely reflect existing EU State aid law practice and are underpinned by a significant enforcement mechanism, thereby providing the EU with the assurance it needed to protect the level playing field. The irony is that the UK was a net beneficiary of the EU system and it was always in its interests to continue benefiting from a set of principles that bound its own spending decisions, as well as those of EU Member States, albeit within a system that offers UK businesses less protection than under EU membership. At the time of writing, the UK was making its first steps towards creating a domestic system of subsidy control. This could provide far greater flexibility than the EU's notification regime, and there are many questions still left unresolved as to how it would operate. There are also two significant risks moving forward. The first is how resilient the TCA would prove in the face of significant subsidy disputes. The second is the significant uncertainty created by the Northern Ireland Protocol. While the UK government was convinced that the application of EU State Aid rules with respect to aid affecting trade between the EU and Northern Ireland would be very limited, the noise coming out of Brussels was very different. The Northern Ireland Protocol may amount to the continued de facto jurisdiction of EU State aid rules over a large number of UK spending decisions. The fact the TCA principles closely mirror EU State aid law will help limit this, but there will likely be a strong political reaction when the Commission seeks to prohibit a British subsidy that the UK government does not consider as affecting Northern Ireland–EU trade. In this respect a strong UK authority that is able to conduct a dual assessment with the European Commission, on the basis of a strong and continued cooperation relationship, may be strongly desirable.

Index

Printed in the United States
by Baker & Taylor Publisher Services